THE
DIVINE–HUMAN ENCOUNTER

By EMIL BRUNNER

Professor of Theology in Zürich

Translated by Amandus W. Loos

PHILADELPHIA

THE WESTMINSTER PRESS

COPYRIGHT, 1943, BY THE WESTMINSTER PRESS

PRINTED IN THE UNITED STATES OF AMERICA

THE TRANSLATOR'S PREFACE

THE striking German title of this short volume, Wahrheit als Begegnung, points to what is central in all of Professor Brunner's writing: his preoccupation with the dimension of the personal.

In these lectures he is talking about what happens when God meets man, the personal encounter between the Creator and the human creature. The central theme of this slim volume can be simply stated: when God meets man, Christian truth comes into being.

Professor Brunner stresses that this dynamic conception of Christian truth is cardinal in the actualistic Biblical point of view as contraposed to the substantialist Greek point of view. Christian truth has to do with something happening: it is (so to say) an act — it is an event. And that event is the personal encounter between God and man. It should perhaps be noted that in translating the word Begegnung as 'encounter' in the title and in some places in the text, the English word is used in the sense which Principal Cairns points out is becoming customary, namely, without any suggestion of hostility being implied.

The translation of these lectures was begun about a year after their delivery in 1937. At that time arrangements were made for publication of the English translation with a British publishing house. With the advent of the war it became necessary to change these plans, and the translation was laid aside. For this reason the translation is appearing some five years after the lectures were delivered in Sweden. It is clear, *however, that the writing has lost none of its contemporaneity or challenge.*

It is my pleasure to thank several people who have helped me in the preparation of this translation. Professor Paul Tillich, of Union Theological Seminary, made a number of illuminating suggestions. My colleague at Spelman College, Dr. Hilda Weiss, has been patient in helping to eliminate Germanisms and to clarify the English text at many points. Professor George D. Kelsey, of Morehouse College, Atlanta, and Miss Abigail Hoffsommer, of the East and West Association, New York City, read the entire manuscript and gave suggestions about the English style. Professor Amos Wilder, of Andover Newton Theological School (now of the Chicago Theological Seminary), checked the transliterations of the Greek words and their translation.

A. W. L.

SPELMAN COLLEGE, ATLANTA, GEORGIA
6 JUNE 1943

FOREWORD

THIS *inquiry into the Christian understanding of truth is a series of lectures, in part considerably revised, which were delivered on the Olaus Petri Foundation at the University of Upsala in the fall of 1937. The suggestion to make the relation between the objective and the subjective in Christian faith the theme of the lectures was given by my friend, Professor A. Runestam, of Upsala, at that time the president of the Foundation. This theme has proved to be an extremely valuable starting point for reflection about the Biblical concept of truth — reflection which led to the insight, important alike for theology and the practical work of the Church, that our understanding of the message of salvation and also of the Church's task is still burdened with the Subject-Object antithesis which originated in Greek philosophy. The Biblical conception of truth is: truth as encounter. Applying this knowledge in all spheres of Church doctrine and practice is of direct and unforeseen import; in this application I am aware that I have made only a modest beginning. But surely I may hope that this first advance will be of interest to all who take seriously the Reformation interpretation of Scripture. If my thesis in these lectures really represents faithfully the Biblical understanding of truth, then indeed much of our thinking and action in the Church must be different from what we have been accustomed to for centuries.*

Since I am convinced of the fallibility of the theological teacher — whoever he may be — I lay these results before my fellow searchers for criticism. But I trust that they will agree with the main points, at least in so far as the Bible itself and not some specific dogma about it is the final authority.

EMIL BRUNNER.

ZÜRICH
MARCH, 1938

CONTENTS

Contents

CHAPTER THREE

Contents

Contents

CHAPTER SIX

CHAPTER ONE

Objectivism and Subjectivism
in the History of Christendom

CHAPTER ONE

••

Objectivism and Subjectivism
in the History of Christendom

W**HENEVER** an individual, a people, or an epoch ceases to take existence merely for granted, two questions at once arise: 'What is truth?' and 'How can we become possessed of the truth which thus is?' The problem, how thinking or knowing is related to being, which more than any other has engaged Western philosophy from its first beginnings down to the present time, is not based upon a misunderstanding as has recently been maintained; it springs necessarily from our very existence. The familiar experience that there may be conflicting opinions concerning the same matter of fact is enough to force upon us the distinction between an objective being and a subjective knowing of that being. Especially in the sphere of science, though by no means only there, the striving for 'objectivity,' for the greatest possible correspondence between 'thinking' and 'being,' is rightly regarded as the one true ideal of the search after knowledge.

We are not concerned here with this general philosophical problem, but only with the relation between the 'objective' and the 'subjective' in Christian faith. The question is theological rather than philosophical, not only in regard to its subject matter but also, and equally, with reference to its presuppositions. We ask not as those who are primarily interested to know if and in what sense there is truth in the Christian faith, but rather as those who, being believing members of the Church, have knowledge of divine truth through the revelation in Jesus Christ. Our question arises, as we are accustomed to say today, from within the Church, not from without, and is intended as a backward-looking inquiry on the part of believers into the source, the foundation and the norm, of their faith — which can be no other than the Word of God become flesh in Jesus Christ.

As men who in him find the truth, we raise the question concerning the relation between the objective and the subjective in Christian faith. But first of all let me explain how I arrived at this statement of the problem and why we may expect it to yield instruction that is not only serviceable to the Church but in the highest sense necessary to it.

The Three Roots of the Theological Task. The task of theology — I am thinking now only of dogmatic and not of historical or exegetical theology — is to attain clarity as to what the Church has to proclaim, what the Christian has to believe, and what the practical consequences of this proclamation and this faith are for the Church and its individual members. This clarity it seeks to attain by means of reflection upon the revelation of God as given us in the Bible. This entire theological task, if I rightly understand the matter, has three different roots in the life of the Church: the exegetical, the didactic, and the polemic. The Christian community needs help in its use of the Bible, and that not only in interpreting single texts or passages, but also in grasping the interconnection, in relating the single concepts to the revelation in its entirety. Thus, for example, the Lutheran dogmatic grew out of Melanchthon's *Theological Common Places,* which in its turn was meant as a guide for the Bible reader. So also the Church has from the first recognized the task of instructing its members in the chief contents of the history of revelation and Holy Scripture in a sort of short compendium or catechism. The main facts and truths which form the foundation of the Christian faith are to be selected as such out of the great wealth of thoughts and occurrences which are crowded into the Bible, and exhibited in a definite, understandable connection to each other. Since, however, there are those among the Church's members who are alive to the thinking and problems of their time and cannot be satisfied with the elementary lessons of the first instruction, there arises the second type of dogmatic theology, as it first took shape in Augustine's handbook and, in monumental form, in Calvin's *Institutes.* Finally the Church since its beginning has had to be on its guard against the corruption of its message by heretics within and opponents without; it has had to oppose false with true Biblical doctrine, proving it to be such from the Scriptures. Inasmuch as this necessary work could be accomplished only through reflection upon the connected whole, there grew out of this root the third type of dogmatic theology, somewhat as it took form in Zwingli's *Commentary on True and False Religion.* It cannot fail to be realized that from this third source of dogmatic theology have come the most powerful, if not always the purest, impulses. Theology therefore is not only (systematized) Bible interpretation, not only (broadened and deepened) instruction, but fundamentally also critical reflection and controversy.

Since heresy all too gladly uses the Bible for its own purposes, its true nature can be exposed only by discovering its basic presuppositions. This controversy and critical self-interpretation [*Selbstbesinnung*] therefore often result in the statement of questions and concepts which are strange to the simple believer and even to the Bible itself — as, for example, those of the doctrine of the Trinity or of the two natures of Christ, or the problem of a principle based on the Bible or a principle derived from tradition. Such questions and concepts are at first rightly held suspect by the community of believers. Since thinking is easier for us than practical obedience in faith and love, the danger of willful speculative developments is always with us, and these lead all too readily and in unforeseen ways to transformations in the Gospel. And indeed the willfulness of speculative theology, whose particular intellectual interests have led it ever farther from the essential Biblical message, has brought heavy losses to the Church both in ancient and modern times. Hence the mistrust of all ideas which are not derived directly from the Biblical world is readily understood and entirely justified.

Yet unfortunately it remains necessary to ask these questions which at first seem alien to the immediate interests of faith, most especially at those points where the proclamation and present faith of the Church have already been molded and transformed, even though unconsciously and in unnoticed ways, by categories of thought to which the Bible itself stands opposed. Such transformations are particularly dangerous and difficult to recognize when they concern, not merely single articles of doctrine, but the whole of it; when they affect, like the sign before an algebraic parenthesis or the constant factors in a physics formula, every single concept of faith. Very early in the history of the Church, for example, the idea arose under the influence of Greek philosophy that the divine revelation in the Bible had to do with the communication of those doctrinal truths which were inaccessible by themselves to human reason; and correspondingly that faith consisted in holding these supernaturally revealed doctrines for truth. This Greek intellectualistic recasting of the understanding of revelation and faith has caused immeasurable damage in the Church to the present day. Yet it can be detected only very indirectly when the approach is from the Biblical point of view, since the entire Bible was written by Hebrews — by men from whom this misunderstanding which runs through all Greek philosophy lay as far distant as it lay close to the Greeks. To track down such a presupposition — foreign, even contrary, to the Bible itself — is therefore as difficult as it is necessary: difficult, because it cannot be discovered in a single article of doctrine but extends through the whole of it; necessary, because it has alienated from its peculiar meaning the entirety of Christian doctrine. The ' sickness,' figuratively speaking, lies not in a localized abscess or in a deformed organ, but rather in the corruption of the blood, which thus secretly spreads the corruption into all organs.

The Biblical Understanding of Truth and the Object-Subject Antithesis. A supposition of this kind — untested and for the most part unrecognized and unconscious — from earliest times has burdened the Church's understanding of revealed truth and has determined its practice. I refer to the application of the antithesis between Object and Subject, between the objective truth of faith (Credo) and the subjective acceptance of faith (credo). At once it seemed possible to place under this general philosophic antithesis the correlation, authoritative for the Biblical message, between the Word of God and faith or between the act of God and the knowledge of faith. For is it not very obvious that the Word of God is what is objectively given, while faith is the subjective appropriation of what is given? Once one is convinced of the legitimacy of this coequalization, I dare say one can and must go farther, and in similar fashion set other objectivities, such as the Church as institution, the Sacraments, or the offices, in contradistinction to the faith of the individual, and likewise confuse the superindividual-collective and the individual-personal with the antithesis between objective and subjective. Questioning these tradition-hallowed forms of thought will doubtless be neither easy nor without danger, since as a rule the greatest controversies, like the most serious errors, occur where attention is focused on such unverified suppositions which are considered self-evident.

In order to be clear from the start about the subject matter of these chapters, I am already indicating the *thesis*, which is to be further explained and justified: *that the use of the Object-Subject antithesis in understanding the truth of faith and* furthermore in the Church generally is by no means self-evident; on the contrary it *is a disastrous misunderstanding* which affects the entire content of Christian doctrine and also operates fatally in the practice of the Church, most severely impairing the proclamation of the Word and faith among the fellowship. *The Biblical understanding of truth cannot be grasped through the Object-Subject antithesis: on the contrary it is falsified through it.* This does not mean, to be sure, that we should avoid using this conception, since it is indispensable for natural-rational knowing, or that we can do without it in every respect; indeed we should have to stop thinking altogether if we entirely gave up using it. This thesis does mean, however, that where the heart of faith is concerned — the relation between God's Word and faith, between Christ and faith — the Objective-Subjective correlation must be replaced by one of an entirely different kind.

The Two Tendencies, Objectivism and Subjectivism, in the History of the Church. In order to clear the way toward an understanding of this thesis, I should like first of all to elucidate briefly several familiar facts in the history of the Church, in which I must make use of the customary terminology, the pair of conceptions just questioned by me, namely, Objective-Subjective. Throughout the entire history of the Church we see two tendencies, Objectivism and Subjectivism, competing with one another. Behind these two terms, which neither the Bible nor the simple believer recognizes, lie facts of the highest importance: errors in faith and in the Church's transactions, corruption of Christian piety and sinful mistakes, which more than once have brought the Christian Church to the very brink of misrepresentation and dissolution.

Two Kinds of Objectivism.   Everyone who in some measure is gripped by the living Biblical faith as the Reformation revived it will be startled to discover the questions raised and answered in an authoritative textbook of Roman Catholic moral theology.   For example, how long after it has been received does the consecrated Host of Christ remain in the stomach of believers?   Shocked, we ask how such a misunderstanding of the holy meal instituted by our Lord could be possible.   We may wonder less, though our astonishment will be no smaller, if we notice that in the same textbook appeal is made for decisions regarding all moral questions to the final authority of the Holy See; and obedient submission to it is inculcated as one of the chief duties of the Christian.   Here too we recognize something wholly foreign to the Biblical kind of faith, an almost inconceivable change in the understanding of the obedience of faith.   But these two and many other facts no less astonishing or weighty, at first seeming to stand alongside each other without any connection, become understandable as symptoms of the self-same ' sickness ' when considered from the point of view of Objectivism.   Both, in fact — this magical-materialistic conception of the Sacrament and this authoritative principle of the obedience of faith, not to mention many other notions in the Roman Catholic theology and Church — have one and the same root, characterized by the catchword, Objectivism. By Objectivism I understand here a tendency of man's spirit and will to get something into his power — to manipulate it like an object in definite ways and within definite limits — something which by its very nature is not under human control. Man habitually exerts himself to build into a system of human assurances something of which he cannot dispose and which in essence is not disposable, such as divine grace and truth. Our Lord gave the Sacrament to His fellowship that in it He might be present to believers, thereby nourishing and strengthening their faith. Yet it was already misinterpreted and changed in the early days of the faith. A free gift of God, an event in which grace and the presence of grace in faith were freely bestowed, became a priestly sacrificial transaction whereby man received into his hand (so to say) the presence and grace of God. With the word of consecration the priest transforms the bread and wine into the body and blood of Christ, thus producing (as it were) salvation like a heavenly medicine — in the second century it was already called the medicine of immortality. Of course he is not allowed to effect the transformation-miracle when and where he will, but he can do it *per nefas*. Salvation is in his — or at least in the Church's — power. A practice wholly impersonal, something physical-metaphysical, has evolved out of an experience wholly personal, out of an event of the kind described by the words, 'Where two or three are gathered together in my name, there am I in the midst of them.' The Host is an object which the priest, or the Church through the priest, produces by virtue of his office and by virtue of a mumbled word — 'the transformation of the elements is not effected by means of the humble, solemn prayer invoking God's

23

Spirit, but by means of the consecration formula spoken by the priest, who is endowed with divine power.' (Heiler, *Der Katholizismus*, p. 224.) And the Church disposes of this object just as it likes, in a way which has at the least a striking similarity to a material medicament. Hence it is really considered an object. From this point of view the question and answer in the book of moral theology mentioned above, at first wholly incomprehensible to us, are understandable at least in their own context.

In the second place Objectivism is of a subtler kind; but the fundamental point of view and tendency, as in the instance of altering the meaning of the Bible, are basically the same. It pleased God to make known to mankind the secret of His Will in Jesus Christ, to reveal Himself in the Incarnate Word. But this revelation, although it was given once for all, remains God's right and God's deed, and hence reserved to Himself alone. It is not and never can become something at man's disposal. The proclamation of the written word is God's Word, wherever and whenever it pleases Him; the word of preaching is recognized as the Word of God only when and because the Holy Spirit gives it to be recognized as such. The human heart must be opened in faith through the power of God's own Spirit if that on which everything depends is to come to pass: the knowing of God. To be sure, the responsibility has been laid upon the Church to proclaim to all the world the message entrusted to it; but it can manifest the Word of God only when that Word is especially given to it. The Word of God is no disposable object, but a free gift of grace. For ' the Spirit bloweth where it list-

24

eth.' The Church ' has ' the Word, and yet it must always receive it anew, if it is actually to proclaim it. The preacher ' has ' his sermon, on paper or in his head; but it can become a mighty deliverance of God's Word only through the gift of God's Spirit — and for that he must constantly make renewed entreaty. This waiting and hoping, this dependence on God's free intervention, is always burdensome and vexing for man. If wholly dependent upon this free intervention of God, the Church is most especially afraid in the life-and-death warfare which it must wage again and again. It would like to hold some assurances in its hand — who could not understand that! It would like to have in its power for disposal that in which lies its stability and its very life. It would like to be certain of God in a more direct way than is guaranteed through the promise as given to faith and in prayer. So the Church built up a mighty apparatus, a system of ecclesiastical assurances, by means of which it might become the power in control of the divine revelation. The authority of the divine Word was seized (so to speak) and made available in an ecclesiastical system of authority. The Church of faith and the free-governing grace of God became the Church of the holy episcopal canon law. The authority of the Word of God was delegated to this legal apparatus of the Church, and the crown of this system of assurances is the Papacy. When the Pope speaks, God speaks: doctrine fixed by the Holy See is divine, revealed truth. *Roma locuta, causa finita* — Rome having spoken, the cause is decided. The erstwhile insecurity of the Church has given way to an impressive, magnificent security, imposing to men of every age. Man now has what he wants. Now he has the divine revelation and also the secure human possession: the invisible and heavenly authority but also the visible and human. He has the Spirit of God and His gifts under his own administration and disposal; when he is ordained, the priest receives the Holy Spirit from the hand of the Church.

What we have seen in these two especially clear examples from the ambit of Roman Catholic doctrine and practice will be observed during the course of this and the following chapters as obtaining within the whole sphere of the Christian Church, in the Protestant no less than in the Catholic. Always and everywhere the same tendency to seek security rises out of man's sinful, anxious nature and therefore expresses itself wherever men have the Church.

Subjectivism in the History of the Church. But this Objectivism has its counterpart — if I may so express it — of equal rank: Subjectivism — rooted as deeply in the being of man and just as devastating in its effect on the Church. The striving for what is fixed, secure, authoritative, and disposable certainly does not hold an uncontested sovereignty; rivaling it is a drive at least as elemental and possibly even more primitive — the urge for freedom and spontaneity. Indeed, the development of systems of authority and assurances is partly a reaction against this unruly, fetter-smashing urge in the individual, which breaks through all fixed order in seeking to attain the highest possible unlimited self-realization. The urge for the adventure of freedom is fully as powerful as that for security, and Biblical doctrine brings it into especially close connection with the very essence of sin. Of this we shall speak in a later context. But the Word of God is first of all a taming of this insubordinate, egoistic desire for freedom. For it is concerned with establishing the sovereignty of God, with the obedience of faith, with the imprisoning of human reason by obedience to Christ, with validating the unconditional authority of God. The Gospel came into the world as the obedience-commanding message of the dominion of God.

But the human heart with its egoistic desire for freedom asserts itself even here — where the Gospel is accepted as well as where it is rejected. The First Epistle of Paul to the Corinthians shows us how the Christian community from its beginnings had to hold off this false desire for freedom: individualistic enthusiasm [*Schwarmgeisterei*] is as old as the Church itself. And *this* is Subjectivism in the Church. To defend itself against this subjective movement which would have undermined its very foundations, the early Church built up a system of assurances. Primarily though not entirely, Objectivism is a reaction to Subjectivism.

In order to prove its ecclesiastical identity, Objectivism clings to the historical givenness of the revelation, to the Word of truth given, spoken, and written once for all: the individualistic enthusiast, on the contrary, insists that everything depends on the free rule of the Spirit. ' The Spirit bloweth where it listeth ' — hence there is nothing fixed, nothing divinely given, no rule and authority, no established doctrine and institution. Nothing is binding but the free, ruling Spirit of God, who enlightens everyone, when and how He pleases. This enlightening through the Spirit takes place, according to this point of view, from moment to moment, without established rules, without being bound to the fixed, given Word or to historical facts. Only the individual can experience it, and only in his solitary experience has he the certainty of the divine revelation. These individualistic enthusiasts have no other criterion or basis for faith than experiencing the impartation of the Spirit. All that is given and established, all fixed doctrine, all ordered office, all ecclesiastical constitution or arrangement — yes, even the fixing of God's Word in the Biblical canon — for them this is at once falsification, torpidity.

Throughout the entire history of the Church movements have arisen in which this claim of the incommunicability of Spirit-enlightenment was defended against all ecclesiastical objectivities. The measure of subjectivity, moreover, is very varied — that is to say, in the radical means whereby this subjective principle of incommunicability is established — very varied in the way in which it reckons with objective ecclesiology, in which it allies itself with or stands against it in secret or open opposition; correspondingly very varied, too, is the reaction of the Church. The history of the sects, the orders, Mysticism, and the group movements of every kind, is filled with accounts of these times of reckoning, both inimical and peaceful. In fact, the changing relations between Objectivism and Subjectivism make up a large part of early, medieval, and modern Church history.

The Dialectic Principle of the Reformation. From the Catholic point of view, determined by the objective idea of Sacraments and Church, the radical revival of Biblical faith which we call the Reformation must be criticized as Subjectivism. In the following chapters I hope it will become clear why this reproach completely misses the mark. For the God-given power of the Reformation lies in the fact that through it the Church was enabled to escape from this fatal antithesis, Objectivism-Subjectivism, and to find the secret of moving both between and beyond these extremes. Its ' epistemological' principle was a dialectic; that is, its form of expression was never the use of one concept, but always two logically contradictory ones: the Word of God in the Bible and the witness of the Holy Spirit, but these understood and experienced, not as a duality, but as a unity. What is of concern is the truth given once for all, the truth of salvation and revelation clearly discoverable and available in the words of the Bible. But this Biblical truth can never be considered as available, willy-nilly, at the command of the Church in doctrine or dogma, but as the Word of the living, present Spirit of God, wherewith the Incarnate Word, Jesus Christ Himself, takes possession of our hearts and Himself makes His home there. This paradoxical unity of Word and Spirit, of historical revelation and God's contemporary presence, of ' Christ for us ' and ' Christ in us ' — this is the secret of the Reformation, of its power to renew Biblical faith and shake off the fetters of a century-long foreign rule, both theological and ecclesiastical. Time and again we are amazed to find, in dealing now with this, now with that, article of faith, that it is Luther who comprehends and brings fresh light: now in the doctrine of penance or of faith, of the Church or the Word of God; now again at a quite unexpected point in regard to Greek Intellectualism, Sacramentalism, the holy canon law, the ecclesiastical legal doctrine; now in hidden Rationalism, Individualism, the secret mystical haughtiness of egoistic enthusiasm. That he could so completely break through the errors of tradition to the fundamental ideas of the Bible always seems puzzling until we discover that it was the self-evident and necessary consequence of his freeing himself from the spell of a single false antithesis which determined the Catholic misunderstanding of the evangelical message as well as that of the individualistic enthusiast — the spell of the Object-Subject antithesis. This liberation enabled him to rediscover the original Biblical understanding of truth.

Objectivism in Orthodoxy. The Church was given this liberating knowledge in its purity for all too short a time. The return to Catholic Objectivism begins already at the close of the Reformation era itself, becoming more marked, however, in the age immediately after it. Even while controversialists were still arguing fiercely against the newly formulated Tridentine Catholic theology, they themselves had already unconsciously reverted in essential points to Catholicism. We call this the age of Protestant Orthodoxy, and that phrase aptly characterizes the very essence of the period. Orthodoxy is one form — indeed the most important — of Objectivism, and hence of objectivistic misunderstanding of the Biblical message. However anti-Catholic it may seem to be in the content of its faith or in its ecclesiastical postulates, Orthodoxy is essentially Catholic because in it the Word of God is again made compassable; and the objective doctrine has become the actual object of faith. But we must not forget that in the age of Orthodoxy as in the pre-Reformation era there existed alongside of or behind all Orthodoxy a genuine, strong, and true Christian faith, such faith as produces 'peace and joy in the Holy Spirit' and 'which proves itself efficacious in love.' The heritage from the Reformation was not simply lost. The consequences of the renewal of faith made themselves further felt in blessed ways — I need only remind you of the glorious treasury of Church hymns, attaining a particular flowering time during this age, and above all of the courage with which the Protestant Churches and Christians under the Cross stood their ground against the brutalities of the counter-Reformation. And yet no one who studies the history of the post-Reformation period can escape the impression: a hoarfrost has fallen, a splendid growth has suddenly become as though cut off and benumbed. The age of Orthodoxy appears like a frozen waterfall — mighty shapes of movement, but no movement. What happened? The paradoxical unity of Word and Spirit fell to pieces; the Scriptures became a gathering of divine oracles, the essence of divinely revealed doctrine. Men *have* God's Word. In the controversy against the Catholic principle of tradition on the one side, and on the other the principle of the Spirit of the individualistic enthusiast together with the newly arising rationalist principle, the temptation could not be withstood to create a system of assurances including the confessional dogma, the notion of verbal inspiration, and the Bible understood as a book of revealed doctrine. The 'paper Pope' stands over against the Pope in Rome; quite unnoticed the position of dependence on the Word of God is usurped by the appeal to pure doctrine, which in turn is made tantamount to the Word of God. This displacement can already be noticed in a decisive way in the Augsburg Confession, even though still hidden by a living understanding of faith. Interest in doctrine more and more arrogates to itself every other interest; the urge for an ever-nicer precision in the formulation of conceptions — the absence of which in the whole Bible is so characteristic — becomes dominant in Church life and leads to endless, even more subtle, doctrinal controversies. Christian love, practical discipleship atrophies. Once let faith and recognition of a system of revealed doctrines become identical, and Christian piety, described in the Bible as 'faith which proves efficacious in love,' is seen in contradistinction to doctrine in the clearest and most definite way. Catechetical instruction becomes the preferred and practically the sole means of educating the younger generation to become Christians. The thoroughly trained theologian becomes the pattern around which the fellowship is supposed to orientate itself as regards the meaning of being a Christian.

The Pietist Reaction. The reaction to this deterioration in the understanding of faith and in the Church could not fail to appear. The counterstroke ensued, as is customary in history, *ex contrario*, in a movement not unjustly called Pietism, which carried in very various degrees the marks of Subjectivism within itself. To be sure, the movement should be understood primarily as a renewed effort to make real the living, Biblical faith; and the appeal to Luther by some of its representatives has far more historical justification than is commonly recognized. Quite apart from its rejuvenation of the dried-up Protestant Church, what Pietism accomplished in the sphere of social amelioration and foreign missions is at least the token of that Spirit which is promised in the Bible to those who truly believe, and is among the most splendid records of achievement to be found in Church history.

That the movement seen as a whole likewise carried within itself the unmistakable features of a one-sided Subjectivism, even as Orthodoxy those of Objectivism, is nonetheless indubitable. Albrecht Ritschl, despite the one-sidedness and mordancy of his judgment, is not incorrect when in Pietism he sees revived the old motives of the medieval Catholic mystic and of the individualistic enthusiast. The experience of the individual moves commandingly into the center of attention; pious feeling, even where theoretically this term was not used, becomes of chief importance. The hymn of that time clearly proves this contention, being a much more authoritative criterion than the theological assurances to the contrary. The comparatively trifling theological contribution of that epoch is also a distinct sign of the deficient understanding of the aim underlying the doctrinal controversies of the Reformation. Once again, as in the best periods of Catholic Mysticism, the chief concern is for the sanctification of the individual, for achieving Christian personality wholly surrendered to God — by which is meant, in the idiom of Catholicism, the attainment of sainthood.

Schleiermacher. A point of view concerning which we shall have more to say later has recently directed attention, with some satisfaction, to the connection between Pietism and the Rationalism of the Enlightenment. This connection is not to be denied; but if the picture of the situation is not to be falsified, it must at once be added that a similar causal connection also obtains between Orthodoxy and this Rationalism. Even as the Pietist Subjectivism in certain extreme characteristics leads through the very heart of the ' inner light ' to the rationalist principle, so the extreme Intellectualism of late Orthodoxy directly prepares the way for the Age of Reason. In the figure of Schleiermacher the Pietism of his home background and the rationalist philosophy of his day are bound together in a remarkable personal ' creative synthesis.' Despite his vehement protests to the contrary, Schleiermacher is rooted solidly in the fundamentals of the Enlightenment. Like the rationalists, he searches behind the positive, historical religions for their common factor and for what at the same time would be for him their normative ' essence,' the ' religion among the religions '; and he considers the Christian as the purest and most perfect form of religion. On the other hand, he is the confirmed opponent of the usual Intellectualism of the Enlightenment and seeks the essence of religion in pious feeling. All revealed truth, in the last analysis, is submerged for him in this mystic feeling of unity over all antitheses. Subjectivism in Christian theology — that is, in the understanding of the Christian faith — enters with him upon a new phase. While most of the medieval mystics, and even more the Protestant Pietists, left the truth of the Word of the Bible unimpeachable and recognized its fundamental meaning for the Church and faith, this can be said to be only seemingly true for Schleiermacher. His subjective interpretation of the faith of the Church, when closely examined, tends to empty it of content completely. The Word is no longer the divine, revealed authority and the foundation of faith, but only the means of expressing that faith. What of truth-content remains in his 'interpretation' of Christian dogma is hard to say. In any event this great thinker who understood how to bring together Pietism, the Enlightenment, and Idealism into a most impressive unity, pointed the way to a distinctive feature of the nineteenth century — the subjective dissolution of theology.

Progressive Subjectivization. Despite the restraining reactions of the confessional orthodox and Biblicist schools of theology, the development of the understanding of faith during the last century on the Protestant basis unmistakably continued to move toward self-dissolution in the sense that it became more subjective. Even the emphasis of Albrecht Ritschl on the historical did not alter the situation, just because his concern was with the history of which man is the subject, not God. The concern was not with God's revelation in His Word, but more and more with religion; not with the great facts of salvation in the Bible, but with 'values' or with inner experiences or adventures; not with the event of redemption, but with the inner life of Jesus and the like; with factors that could be the objects of a religious psychology, possibly of a transcendental doctrine of the a priori, but not with the miracle of the Word of God becoming incarnate in Jesus Christ, the Mediator. It was reserved for the American ' theology ' in several of its schools of psychology of religion, however, to carry this tendency to a sort of ultimate extreme, so that in the Chicago school, for example, not much more was left of ' religion ' than a certain social feeling or value experience, for the truth content of which it was wholly meaningless to ask. Even if Continental theology never went to such an extreme, a leading spirit such as Troeltsch was a warning sign that Protestantism was not very far distant from a skeptical self-dissolution.

Recent Theological Reflection and the New Objectivism. At this time the war broke out and swept away, together with so much that had become rotten, this hollowed-out, this empty theology. From various sides a powerful reaction set in. Luther was again remembered, and advance from him was made to a new understanding of justifying faith — an understanding born out of the need of the time. The Bible was again made the center for orientation; and, paradoxically enough, it was just out of the radical, final phase of the higher Biblical criticism, out of the results of the so-called eschatological school, that the entirely new impulse arose to take the Biblical message in earnest. The decisive opponent of the Subjectivism of the past generation arose in the ' dia-

lectic theology.' Finally the understanding of the basic Biblical revelation — that understanding which earlier Biblicist
theologians of every current of thought had obstinately defended or discovered anew as an integral part of the Biblical
knowledge of faith, but which because of the presumptive
strength of this trend toward Subjectivism had had little influence — all at once produced unexpected results. Suddenly
men like Kähler and Schlatter, hardly taken into account before the war, became recognized leaders. The theme of ' religion' disappeared. People were allowed and wanted to
hear again about the saving revelation of the Bible, of Jesus
Christ, the Mediator of the divine covenant of grace. For
once the age of Subjectivism, at least for theology, was past.
The Church as recipient and proclaimer of the Word of God
was again taken seriously.

But when the Church is taken seriously, its shadow also
immediately appears again: Objectivism. We have already
seen that particularly during times of controversy, when the
Church as a whole must defend itself against a menacing power
which threatens its very existence, the temptation becomes
strong to imprison the Word of God in a system of human
assurances. Men want to hold something solid in the hand
(so to speak) with which to fight. In controversy, especially with strong forces from without, there is little time
for critical self-interpretation. Massive formulas are needed.
The opponent must be met on terms more or less even. The
tendency to make political both the theological conceptions
and the bearing of the Church is clamant and, humanly
speaking, entirely understandable. But the means used is

orthodox theology, confessional Orthodoxy. It is the product of the tendency toward security, the expression of the determination once for all to secure from every attack the essence of the Church. The ready-made concepts of confessional Orthodoxy are much better suited as weapons of attack and defense than the dialectically oscillating and organic-parabolic notions in the Bible itself. Quite unnoticed, a neo-Orthodox theology shapes itself out of the earlier dialectic, and it carries all the characteristic marks of Objectivism: one-sided emphasis on doctrine, identification of doctrine with the Word of God, overvaluation of the formulated creed, of dogma; one-sided prominence given to the objective factor in preaching, in the understanding of the Church, especially from the point of view of doctrine, Sacrament, and office — and not to the fellowship of believers; the Church considered as institution; neglect of love in favor of Orthodoxy, of practical discipleship in favor of a strict churchly attitude; misunderstanding of the missionary and pastoral task of the Church as the result of a one-sided estimation of the sermon as the didactic expounding of the Bible, and so forth.

Perhaps it would be more correct to speak of this theological, ecclesiastical Objectivism, not as being already present, but rather as in the process of becoming of considerable importance. In any event let us not speak down from any kind of safe bulwark to those who stand in a hard, brave battle and for that reason let themselves be pushed in this direction — thus spoiling the joy of the fighting with the cheap criticism of a spectator. On the contrary, we observe with joy that within the ranks of the bravest the demand for renewed reflection, the warning against overconfidence in the confessional formula, is making itself distinctly heard. But we should not forget that theological movements, once started, follow their own law and produce specific effects of their own even when quite separated from the original controversial situation. It is upon us who do not as yet have a part in this struggle with the beast out of the pit that the double duty is laid to use for very earnest reflection the respite allowed us, on the one hand in order to be better able to help those who are in the combat, on the other to prepare ourselves for the conflict which will also come to us, though probably in quite a different way. The defensive combat that is the brave defense of the Gospel proclamation and the Church clearly is not the only duty ordained for us. For we are summoned to proclaim the Gospel to all creatures, to make disciples of all peoples. But classical Orthodoxy did not have missionary strength and did not create any missionary impulse.

The Necessary Reminder About the Word of God. I hope it has become somewhat clear in this hurried historical sketch that the concern of our day is not to avoid the Scylla of an already existing Orthodoxy only to give way to the Charybdis of a new Pietism. For the grave injustice which undoubtedly has been done Pietism during the past twenty years, I feel it a duty, as one of those more or less responsible, to make some amends. It is precisely we — the group of ' dialectic ' theologians who several years back still enjoyed some unity in being fellow combatants — who have every reason to remember Pietism with the highest gratitude. For the best which we had when we started we were indebted, humanly speaking, to two great figures of Pietism, Chr. Blumhardt in Boll and Kierkegaard, the man who, likewise in conflict against a false Objectivism, ventured the daring sentence: Subjectivity is truth. But it is not and should not be for nothing that we also saw clearly the dubious aspects of Pietism, just this Subjectivism; hence our watchword can be none other than, '*Beyond Orthodoxy and Pietism, Biblical faith!*'

For this reason it is the urgent imperative of the hour to search, by means of reflection about the Word of God itself, for this 'beyond' of Objectivism and Subjectivism which is the secret of true Christian faith. Quite naturally the first thought is that the truth must lie somewhere in the middle, like the arithmetical mean between two ultimate values. The task for the exponent of Objectivism as of Subjectivism, according to this view, would be for each to help the other toward a true evaluation and thereby to a correct delimitation of his own position: this is the expedient of mediation. But one glance at history, specifically at the Reformation, makes this way appear like a feeble compromise which only obscures the real problem but does not solve it. There is no right middle way between Objectivism and Subjectivism: there is no correct mean between two errors. In this instance too the truth is more parodoxical and harder to find. It is not possible to plead the case too strongly for either the so-called objective or subjective element in faith. The more the one is stressed, the more valid the other becomes. But actually the use of the either-or formula is itself false.

With this I come back to the thesis suggested at the beginning of this chapter. In any event the damage to the Church did not lie in the one-sided emphasis on either the objective or the subjective, but rather in the fact that the Biblical revelation was brought under this antithesis. The Bible is as little concerned with objective as with subjective truth. The Objective-Subjective antithesis cannot be applied to the Word of God and to faith. It is a category of thought wholly foreign, not only to the way of expression in the Bible, but also to the entire content. To remove it from the understanding of God's Word and faith is the purpose of these chapters. Through what has already been said I hope that I have indicated to some extent that this thesis is really significant and of importance for the Church. Above all, however, I am anxious to show in the following chapters how through eliminating this tradition-hallowed but devastating prejudice, Biblical truth rises to a new splendor.

CHAPTER TWO

The Biblical Understanding of Truth

CHAPTER TWO

The Biblical Understanding of Truth

The source and norm of all Christian theology is the Bible. Its subject matter is the secret and, at the same time, manifest meaning of the Bible: the God who inclines Himself toward man and makes Himself present to man: Jesus Christ and His Kingdom. This is the presupposition (never to be lost from sight) for my attempt to work out the opposition between the Biblical understanding of truth and the general, rational understanding of truth as determined by the Object-Subject antithesis. This understanding of truth is nowhere explained in the Bible. Even if we brought together and analyzed exegetically all the Biblical passages in which the word 'truth' occurs, we should be hardly a step nearer our goal. Just as the Bible explicates no 'principle of interpretation' and contains no 'doctrine of the Word of God,' so we search it in vain for a 'doctrine of truth.' The more formal a theological concept is, the less it can be directly discovered in or directly validated by the Bible itself. Formal theological concepts are attempts to lay hold of the hidden presuppositions, so to say, the structural form of the Biblical revelation. The passages in which the Bible speaks specifically of the Word of God are proportionately scarce; and yet everything in the Biblical revelation is determined by the category of the Word

45

of God. God is the kind of God who reveals Himself in the Word, even as He also creates and sustains the world through the Word. The task of theology is to elaborate what is formal and at the same time to place it in such a relation with the central contents of the Biblical revelation that it becomes clear how this structural ' form ' is determined by the ' matter ' and the ' matter ' by the ' form.' The God of the Bible is a God who speaks, and the Word of the Bible is the Word of this God. The ' formal principle,' the Word of God, and the ' material principle,' redemption through Jesus Christ or justification by faith alone, are not two but one and the same principle seen in two aspects. Similarly in the following chapters what we hope to work out as the Biblical understanding of truth is not different from what is the concern of the Bible itself; and the formal nature of the concept ' understanding of truth ' and other similar concepts may not be understood as if they pointed to a priori, general epistemological or ontological categories interpreted into the Bible from outside. On the contrary, they are taken from nothing but Scripture itself and stand in the closest connection to all its central contents (as we shall see in later chapters). They are in fact none other than these very contents, considered in their formal aspect, which as such are never directly mentioned in the Biblical word.

The Biblical revelation in the Old and New Testaments deals with the relation of God to men and of men to God. It contains no doctrine of God as He is in Himself [*Gott-an-sich*], none of man as he is in himself [*Menschen-an-sich*]. It always speaks of God as the God who approaches man

46

[*Gott-zum-Menschen-hin*] and of man as the man who comes from God [*Menschen-von-Gott-her*]. That God — even in His ' I-am-ness ' [*An-sich-Sein*] — wishes from the first to be understood as the God who approaches man is precisely the meaning of the doctrine of the Triune God; that man, even in his natural being, is always the man who comes from God is the meaning of the doctrine of the image of God and of original sin. And both are known in their fullness only in Jesus Christ, in whom as the incarnate Son of God both the God who approaches man and the man who comes from God are revealed.

This last suggestion leads naturally to another: that in the Bible this two-sided relation between God and man is not developed as doctrine, but rather is set forth as happening in a story. The relation between God and man and between man and God is not of such a kind that doctrine can adequately express it in abstract formulas, as it is possible to express abstractly, for instance, the relation between the radius and the circumference of a circle or the relation between the Beautiful and the Good. It is not a timeless or static relation, arising from the world of ideas — and only for such is doctrine an adequate form: rather the relation is an event, and hence narration is the proper form to describe it. The decisive word-form in the language of the Bible is not the substantive, as in Greek, but the verb, the word of action. The thought of the Bible is not substantival, neuter and abstract, but verbal, historical and personal. Its concern is not with a relation which exists in and for itself, but with a relation which (so to say) occurs. God ' steps ' into the world, into relation with men:

He deals with them, for them, and in a certain sense also against them; but He acts always in relation *to them,* and He always *acts.*

Similarly, men are also considered as those who are not something in and for themselves, but only as those who from the first are placed in a specific relation to God and then also place themselves in such a relation: either positive or negative, obedient or disobedient, true or false, comformable to God or impious. They too are always considered as those who act: and their action, whether expressing sin or faith, is always understood as action in relation to God.

The God of Man and the Man of God. The God of the Bible is always the God of man, and for that reason is not less but more exalted than the God of the philosophers or mystics. He is never other than the God of man. That is to say, from the first He is that God who ' hath in these latter days spoken unto us by the Son,' in the Incarnation of the Son of God; the God who is concerned about His sovereignty over and fellowship with man, so that whenever one thinks of God he thinks at the same time of His will for mankind. Similarly *man in the Bible is always the man of God* — and therefore not less but much more human than the man of the philosophers. He is never other than the man of God, even though he be also sinner, impious, or forsaken and repulsed by God. Even hell itself is only hell because it is hell in relation to God. What actually happens in this relation of God to man and of man to God makes up the content of the Bible.

But this relation, although two-sided, does not have equal

or interchangeable terms. More correctly it is one-sided in that it originates with God. The initiative in this relationship is taken by God, and only in a secondary way does man have any initiative in it at all. The relation of God to man is always first, that of man to God second and consequent upon the first. Hence the relation of God to man is wholly other than that of man to God. The relation of God to man is clearly primary, creative, and without presuppositions. The relation between God and man could not possibly be stipulated by any impulsion from the human side. God's relation to man has no sort of presupposition in a relation of man to God. On this point there is basic opposition between the Biblical and the idealist, pantheist, and mystical thought of God. Clearly God is first. He paints His image of man on the canvas of nothingness, as it were: and there he stands, a man. God calls man into existence out of nothingness — even though in doing so He uses material which He has prepared previously. And, contrariwise, man's relation to God is secondary: it is consequent upon and determined by the already existing relation between God and man, established through no human effort. The relation between God and man is thus always reciprocal, yet never interchangeable like the relation between left and right. God is always and inconvertibly the first, man always and inconvertibly the second in this relation.

What Happens in the Relation Between God and Man. The Bible teaches about this God and this man, and about this *indissoluble two-sided, yet never interchangeable and in a specific sense one-sided, relation between them.* God is known in His relation to man, we are told; and likewise man comes to know himself in his relation with God. Three factors closely connected with what has already been said about this knowledge need to be pointed out. First is the way in which this knowing and being known finds expression: that the relation of man to God is secondary, not primary. That is, man can know God only as God gives Himself to be known: this is the fundamental Biblical point of view. In a later connection we shall understand that the Bible even makes the further assertion that man can know God only because and in so far as he is known by God. To such a large extent emphasis is placed in the Bible upon the unconditional priority of God in the relation between God and man. The second factor is contained in the first: this knowing is therefore an event, an act. God gives Himself to be known, He reveals Himself, He communicates Himself. On the basis of this revelatory happening or act, man can also know God and his relation to Him, which is itself established by God. Man, moreover, also gains this knowledge in an event, in an act of decision. The unconditional priority of God and the active nature of this knowing are linked together, as can be seen when contrasted with the idealist, mystical teaching. In this teaching the priority of God, this unlikeness between the divine and human subject, does not obtain, but rather an emphasis on the interchangeability, so to say, of the two parties in the relation. Hence knowledge is not an event, but something timeless, a static 'knowing' in which the actual emerges out of the potential by sheer chance. In the Idealist-

Mystic teaching knowledge is neither revelation nor decision, but a perception of something which was always 'there,' ready to be perceived.

The third factor is already indicated in the second: this revelation is itself the decisive element in the act of relation between God and man, is indissolubly connected with it. It is not true that first of all there is a relation between God and man, between man and God, which can be known even though it does not become actual. As a matter of fact, it is precisely in God's giving Himself to be known and in this knowledge of God that the essence of the relation between God and man lies. God meets men so vitally in this relation that they ought to know Him. The revelation of God to men is the decisive element in what God does for them. And on the other hand the knowledge of God is the decisive element in the relation to be realized between man and God. God is the God who approaches man just because and in so far as He reveals Himself; and man is the man who comes from God because and in so far as he knows God on the basis of His revelation. God is always the One who destines man for and calls man to Himself; and man is always the one so destined and called by God. The event which is the relation between God and man hence is always an act of revelation: likewise the event which is the relation between man and God is always a relation based on knowing. For this reason the content of the Scriptures, as narration about this relation which is established from God manward and from man God-ward, is always a history of revealing and knowing. Even the narration of the Bible itself is an integrating element in this history, in which the relation of God manward and of man Godward is realized. Thus the narration of the Bible is not something to be added as ordinarily the story is added to the event — we think of the complaint of the epic singer, that he could ' only ' tell what the heroes had actually ' done.' No, the Biblical narrative itself is a part of the history in which God makes actual His relation to man, in which His Kingdom is realized. It cannot be otherwise, for that which is most essential in the ultimate goal of this history, in the Kingdom of God, is the seeing of God face to face, that ' knowing even as we are known.'

God Creates a Counterpart, Face to Face with Himself. It will be of value to examine even more closely this relation between God and man. First of all we must note that God creates for Himself a person as a counterpart of Himself. This decisive affirmation we make in the sentence from the Apostles' Creed, ' I believe in God, the Father Almighty, maker of heaven and earth '; we assert that God wants and creates and endows an actual counterpart who therefore is not Himself and yet who exists only because God so wills it. In this way Biblical faith in God is differentiated from all Pantheism.

There are trends of thought in Biblical faith which seem to lead to the very edge of Pantheism — for instance, the thought of the divine omnipotence, the all-efficiency, the all-determining decree, and the like. But the boundary is never crossed: the world and, above all, man stand ' over against ' God and can never be identified with Him. God wills it thus

Himself, He has Himself thus arranged it, and He would not change it through all eternity. He gives His creature being, face to face with Himself — indeed, not an independent but a dependent-independent being. God endows the creature with the power to *be* ' over against ' Him — indeed, the power to keep his own being face to face with Him.

To what extent this holds for subhuman nature it is hard to say, since we know it only from the outside. Nor is it of particular importance. In the Bible the subhuman creature (together with certain superhuman powers) is only frame and setting for what takes place between God and man. It has no right to an independent significance for reasons that are yet to be discussed. But the human creature is endowed by God with independent being. The dependence upon God of this creaturely being is, through God's ordinance, of such a kind that at the same time it is always freedom. God places Himself face to face with a free being. Every form of Determinism, any thinking whatsoever which questions or completely denies human freedom, is wholly foreign to the Old and New Testaments; and the fact of man's slavery to sin (of which I shall speak more fully later) should never have become confused with it. Determinism, through Augustine having found its way into Reformation theology, has a Stoic and not a Biblical origin. The Bible speaks of only one relation between God and man, in which man by virtue of God's will and God's creation has a decisively free, independent being, not only toward other creatures, but even toward God Himself. Hence when one believes (as has often happened and is still happening on the grounds of Protestant theology) that to uphold the honor of God he must belittle man's independence and freedom or even defend Determinism, he does not serve the God who has revealed Himself to us in the Holy Scriptures, but rather an abstract, philosophical idea of God. Why so much emphasis falls upon the human creature's independence, which stems from the Biblical idea of God, shall be indicated immediately.

But first of all let us note the other side. This autonomy of man is never independence from God; contrarily, man's freedom is grounded precisely in his dependence on God, so that a maximum of freedom is at the same time a maximum of dependence. Man is the more free, the more he is conscious of his dependence on God and the more dependent he makes himself; the less free, the more he denies this dependence and seeks to withdraw himself from it. Being and knowing are here inextricably intertwined. But it is never true that apparent independence means actual independence. On the contrary. The very man who questions his dependence on God draws every breath (so to say) by leave of the Creator whom he denies. True humanness and true freedom, however, both of which are lost by the man emancipated from God, are present only when man knows and acknowledges his complete dependence on God. Complete dependence on God is at the same time true freedom. In this way Christian thought is delimited from all Deism, which stresses the autonomy of the creature in such a way as to destroy the very concept of creature. God places ' over against ' Himself a real counterpart, a creature of such a nature that he can say 'no' to God, but a creature who in the very act of saying 'no' loses his true strength and freedom.

Lordship and Fellowship. The enduring basis for these assertions must become apparent as a result of more closely examining the nature of the relation between God and man. As yet we have considered this relation only formally, in order first of all to let its structure as such stand out in relief. But only when we have clothed this skeleton with the contents belonging to it can we recognize the message of the Bible in our train of thought. The relation between God and man, with which the Bible is always concerned and which in fact is the single theme in the entire Biblical proclamation, can be stated in two words: *Lordship* and *fellowship*. The pivotal point in the Bible is the concept 'Kingdom of God,' a dual notion holding within itself the ideas of God's being and becoming Lord over men and His fellowship with them; from beginning to end, from the first chapter of Genesis to the last chapter of Revelation, this is the pivotal point around which all else turns. These two ideas of Lordship and fellowship must now be examined more carefully for their exact meaning. Through them we shall find determined the whole of Biblical doctrine, and with it what is our particular aim, the specific Biblical understanding of truth.

What do we mean when we say, 'God is Lord'? First of all simply that God can do what He wills with what He has created. Face to face with his Creator, man has no right and also no power which has not been bestowed upon him by

God. In the concept of Lordship the complete dependence of the creature thus finds a definite expression. To declare that God is Lord is basically nothing other than to take with entire seriousness the idea of creation. That God really is Creator means that the creature has neither right nor power that is not derived from God. This holds for every creature.

But something distinctive obtains for man which really first gives the concept 'Lord' its complete Biblical meaning and its positive content. For the assertion that the creature has no right or power that does not come from God is first of all a negative designation. But God wills to be Lord not only 'over' man: he wills to be Lord 'of' man. God is Lord 'over' clouds and winds, over plants and animals, over galaxies and over atoms. But God is not 'their' Lord. That God is Lord means either that He *wills* to be known and acknowledged by man or that He *is* known and acknowledged by man as the One to whom man unconditionally belongs. Because God wills to be and can be Lord only in this way, He places Himself face to face with an independent creature. For only an independent creature can know and acknowledge. God wills to be acknowledged as Lord in freedom, since it is by virtue of such free acknowledgment that He is Lord in the highest sense. Because so much worth and stress is laid upon the Lordship of God in the Biblical revelation, so much stress must be placed in the Bible on the independence of man. The emphasis upon independence hence has nothing to do with the freedom-of-the-will motif of Greek or modern Humanism. It is, if I may so express it, a theocratic Humanism.

God places a creature face to face with Himself, a creature who in having the power of knowing and acknowledging has a share in the essential nature of God, namely, in being a subject. Perhaps we shall also have to concede that in sub-human nature — but in a much weaker and more indistinct sense — there is something of the nature of being a subject; but in the sense of free knowing and acknowledging, in the sense of voluntary subordination of the creation under the Creator, man alone of all created beings known to us is suited to be a subject. Because the will to Lordship is inextricably linked with the nature of God (that nature as known to us in His revelation), God as we said right at the start is always the God who approaches man. And because this subjectivity of man is, according to the revelation of the Bible, exclusively grounded in God's will to Lordship, man is always the man who comes from God.

Perhaps it is possible to imagine a merely reflecting subjectivity, that is to say, a consciousness which is related to its counterpart like a mirror to its reflection. It is even possible to think that such a consciousness would reflect God's Lordship as a mirror reflects what stands before it. Indeed we even possess in a certain sense this mirrorlike subjectivity, especially when we receive within ourselves impressions of objects in a completely disinterested way, involuntarily, and in entire passivity. With such a mirrorlike or echolike counterpart God is not concerned; for thereby His will as Lord is not sufficiently exalted. In freedom, in free decision, in self-sacrifice, He wills to be known and acknowledged as Lord by His counterpart. He is concerned about the free obedience of

His creatures. Because in the full sense God can be Lord only of such a subject who in free personal decision acknowledges Him as Lord, He wills this independence of the creature in the very same unconditional way that He wills to be Lord. From this consideration we can see how fundamentally the God who reveals Himself to us in the Bible is misunderstood if one believes that he must exalt the divine omnipotence and absoluteness at the cost of human freedom and independence. It is decisively Biblical that in the knowledge of God His omnipotence and absoluteness are maintained together with this freedom of His creaturely counterpart, and every attempt to deny this face-to-face relationship for the sake of a supposed exalting of the divine omnipotence will be rejected. Not the *Deus absolutus* — that ' God ' to which an abstract philosophical thinking leads — but the Lord our God, whose Will it is to be Lord in a Kingdom of God, is the ' God of Abraham, Isaac and Jacob,' the ' Father of our Lord Jesus Christ.' That the creature can be in freedom ' over against ' God is grounded in the Will of God to be Lord, and man's unconditional interest in God is given with and grounded in his unconditional interest that God may be Lord.

This is the concrete meaning of our purely formal opening statement, that the Bible says nothing of a God as He is in Himself and nothing of a man as he is in himself, but only of a God who from the first is related to man and of a man who from the first is related to God, and, indeed, in such a way that in this relation God is inconvertibly the first, man inconvertibly the second. This is to say that God is the

Creator-Lord and man is the creature, created to be freely obedient. The Biblical revelation of God shows us this and no other God, and God wills to be called by this and no other name: the Lord who in a freely obedient mankind wills to realize His Lordship, the God of the Kingdom of God. Nowhere is the Bible concerned with an abstract divine omnipotence and an abstract absolute. To be sure no obliterating of the boundary, no equalization of any sort between God and man, is suggested when we say that the independent freedom of the human creature is to be maintained as unconditionally as the Lordship of God; for this free selfhood of man is grounded only in God's will and Creator-power, and his self-realization depends entirely on the acknowledgment of this absolute dependence on God's will and power. God alone is the source of man's being and freedom, and God's *Will* and *creation* is indeed this source, not some eternal timeless emanation or essential interrelatedness. But as certainly and unconditionally as God wills to be Lord, so certainly and unconditionally He wills to have His free counterpart. Whoever therefore abandons this unambiguous but double-sided basic relation for the sake of an ostensibly higher, holier notion of God may be concerned about God's being taken more absolutely and more seriously. Actually he is thus interpreting the omnipotence and all-efficiency of God as sole-efficiency and so canceling out the true face-to-face relation. In this way he veritably destroys the Biblical thought of God.

The second concept by which this formal two-sided relation is made concrete is that of *fellowship*. Above all and in a unique way God wills to have fellowship with His human creatures. This second concept emphasizes the first; but the first is fulfilled only in the second. We have just said that God creates a counterpart who in freedom acknowledges Him as Lord, but God does this in order that He may communicate with this creature in love. He wills not only that His creation shall acknowlege Him as Lord and obey Him, but that it will love Him with the love which He gives to that creation. In this relation too God intends to be unconditionally first. In contrast to all Platonic or Neoplatonic *eros*, God's freely given love is first, man's love for God is always a reciprocated love — is second and is consequent upon the first. Similarly, man in loving is unconditionally dependent upon God. This love is completely grounded in God's will and act; but it is nonetheless the free, spontaneous love of the creature.

If God's will to Lordship is His *self-affirmation* ' over against ' and in the creature, then His love — His will to fellowship — is His unconditional *self-communication* to the creature. God as Lord wills to be loved; obedient acknowledgment of the divine Lordship is the essential presupposition of love for God. But love for God cannot be grounded in His Lordship by itself, but only in such a kind of Lordship in which He communicates Himself. Man can unconditionally love only the unconditionally loving God. The relation of the fulfilled condition thus subsists between Lordship and obedience on the one hand, and between self-communication and responding love on the other. This must be understood in greater detail.

First of all, it is clear that what was said about acknowledgment of God as Lord holds good especially for love: love presupposes complete freedom. Enforced love is not love at all. To be anything else except free contradicts the nature of love — precisely that love depicted in the Bible as the right kind of love. Love presupposes an even higher degree of freedom than the acknowledgment (in obedience) of God as Lord. Love is the most freely willed of any activity of which we are able to think. Love is actually the essence of free will, and contrariwise the essence of free will is love. Hence love is the very opposite of all involuntary, disinterested reflex subjectivity, of which we were speaking above — the subjectivity that is turned toward an object as a mere object. We shall soon see what sort of significance this factor has for the Biblical conception of truth. Love is the most active and most personal of anything of which we can think. For this reason the Bible always speaks of 'hearty' love. In love the whole person freely gives himself.

But love is not only the most completely free, but at the same time the most completely dependent. Whilst we are loving God — in the sense in which the Bible speaks of love for God — we know ourselves to be (as indeed we are) unconditionally dependent upon God, upon His giving love. Our creaturely love can be nothing other than the free return of that which God has first given us, of that which God in His love gives us — that is Himself and therewith our actual life. We can give ourselves to God in love only because He has given Himself to us. If already in the recognition of the Lordship of God our unconditional dependence upon God is known and acknowledged, this knowledge and acknowledgment is fulfilled in the love which is the answer to His freely given love — the love freely given without necessity. For this reason the Lordship of God — the dominion or Kingdom of God — first comes to fulfillment in this responding love.

God wills to be Lord; the *Gloria Dei* shall be reflected in men: this is the dominion, the Kingdom of God. He can be Lord in the perfect sense only when He finds the fullest devotion given to Him by those who have the fullest freedom, that is to say, in love. Similarly, it is true that His Lordship fulfills itself in His sovereign Creator-freedom, that without necessity He gives being to His creature, so that in His giving the creature has life. The self-communication of God is the unconditional Lordship of God: even while God is communicating Himself to the creature, He attains self-realization in the highest sense, His *Gloria.* For this reason His self-affirmation fulfills itself in His self-giving, His glory as Lord in the choir of those who lovingly worship Him as the inconceivably loving Lord. Thus God's will to Lordship — His holiness — points to His will to self-communication, His love in which His holiness is fulfilled; and His love points back to His will to Lordship as its presupposition.

But this is not to be understood as if in the final analysis Lordship or the holiness of God could be reduced to His love, so that it would suffice to speak about God's love. Not without reason the Bible time and again speaks of both as of two very different things. We cannot rightly understand the love of God — that is to say, understand it as freely giving love — if we do not understand it as the love of Him who unconditionally wills to be Lord; nor can we rightly understand His Lordship in any ultimate sense if we do not understand it in relation to His loving Will. Both exist necessarily alongside each other, yet not foreign to one another but one in reference to the other. In both, however, as Lord and as the boundlessly loving One, in His demand for obedience and in His self-communication, God is known as originally relating Himself to a creature who is His counterpart, who in freedom returns what God has previously given him. It is thus with reference to the love of God (that love in which and as which God has revealed Himself to us) that we first understand in the full sense what it means that God is the God who approaches man and man is the man who comes from God.

Revelation and Knowledge of God. A further twofold factor can be understood at this point. Self-revelation and knowing, as we have said from the start, is always the decisive element in the God-man relation. Now we can understand why this is true: because God wills to be *known* as Lord. It does not satisfy Him to be Lord over man as He is Lord over the subhuman creatures. He wills to be their Lord because only in His being *known* as Lord *is* He really Lord in the complete sense.

God is certainly also Lord over those who do not know Him or obey Him or love Him — yet not in the full sense as when He is known as Lord. This is first really true in regard to fellowship. In some way God no doubt also has fellowship with the subhuman creatures whose life is derived from

Him without their knowing it. With them too He is, after all, the loving Giver, but not in the full sense.

He is loving Giver in the full sense less than ever when the human creature does not respond to His love. In this latter instance His fellowship with the creatures can reveal and realize itself only as His wrath, in that He holds them fast even in their rebellion against Him. Yet in that relation He can never give Himself in the true sense of His will to fellowship. Fellowship with God is present only when the creature meets His love with responding love, when the creature knows and appropriates His freely giving love.

Thus the knowledge, and the revelation in which the knowledge is rooted, is the decisive element as much in the Lordship as in the self-communication of God. Heat and motion can be communicated without revelation and knowledge, but not Lordship and the will to fellowship. The Lordship and love of God can be communicated in no other way than by His giving Himself to be known and by His becoming known. Responding love in essence means nothing else than that freely given love is recognized for what it is. In the final analysis existence *in* love and knowledge *of* love are the same.

Perhaps we should be more accurate to say (and this is the second point) that knowledge and act, knowing and *happening*, are in this instance a single process. God communicates Himself in love: and this happens in the fullest sense only when His love is known in responding love. Unless this happening takes place, self-communication cannot consummate itself. It does not reach its goal. This act of divine self-communication thus brings together within itself the dual event of revelation and knowledge. In the responding love of the human creature the will of God is first realized: in the ' yes ' to the self-giving love of God fellowship first takes its rise. The factor of knowledge thus belongs as the decisive factor to the act of self-communication.

All the formal concepts laid down earlier to characterize the divine-human relation have now been given their concrete content. Only in this way do they become intelligible in their essential interrelationship. This interrelationship is not a priori but of course entirely a posteriori, that is to say, grounded in God's act of self-communication. Since God's being as the Bible reveals it to us in no sense is being as such [*An-sich-Sein*] but will to Lordship and will to fellowship therefore it is essentially a related being — a being related to man, the creature who knows, acknowledges, obeys, and loves — a being related to the Kingdom of God. Because God is necessarily first and man second, the being of the creature, especially of the human creature, is receptive and rooted in the divine acting. Because God's will is both will to Lordship and will to fellowship, He wills to have a creature face to face with Himself who in freedom gives back to Him what He first gives to him. Therefore the act in which man receives the being to which God has determined him is an act of revelation and knowledge. Finally, this free face-to-face relation of God and the creature is essentially and necessarily grounded in the divine will to Lordship and fellowship. Consequently it participates in the unconditioned character of the divine will.

God is thus the God who approaches man and man is the

65

man who comes from God, in order that God's will may fulfill itself in man's knowing and voluntary loving and that man's true life may be realized in his voluntarily acknowledging and affirming the divine acting and will. This two-sided but unambiguous relation, this state of the dependent-independent creature — to be face to face with God according to His Will — is the fundamental category of the Bible; and in relation to it everything said in the Bible is said and must be understood. All that the Bible has to say about God's being and doing, about time and eternity, about the divine purpose and creation, about sin and redemption, about grace and works, about faith and penance, about Church and Sacrament, is said within this basic structure and also formulates in a specific way this basic relation. Thus everything that theology avers must remain within this basic structure and everything that contradicts this fundamental presupposition must be rejected and fought against as an un-Biblical and even anti-Biblical error of speculation or doctrinal distortion. We call this basic formal relation, which at the same time is identical with the contents of the whole Bible, *personal correspondence*. What the Bible calls ' truth ' can somehow be derived from these statements. But it must be explained more completely and more exactly with respect to the epistemological problem of truth.

The Word and the Faith. Two concepts which are constitutive for personal correspondence have not yet been specifically mentioned: *the Word* and *the faith*. Of course, implicitly they were always presupposed. Revelation and knowledge belong in essence, as we saw, to the relation between God and man. God as Lord lays claim to the obedience of man; and in revealing Himself as the God of love, He gives His love to man for the sake of and within man's responding love. He does both through His Word. For the Word is the way in which mind communicates with mind, subject with subject, will with will. The Word, on the other hand, is that communication which does not convert the subject into an object; but when it is accepted it stimulates self-activity. The Word is the self-communication of God, which reserves an area of freedom for creaturely self-decision, which gives without violence, which so gives that the taking can be self-giving, voluntary self-giving.

The secret of the person is disclosed through the Word, in him who addresses as well as in him who is addressed. Only the Word is able to break through the infinite strangeness and the silent seclusion between persons: the Word unlocks person to person. But not the word of man: only the Word of God can accomplish this — why and how will be discussed later. In this place the only point to be made is that God's self-communication is made by the Word — a self-communication which at the same time reveals to man God's Lordship and Love, in such a way that he acknowledges and accepts them. Since, therefore, the Word is the form and the means through which person reveals and gives himself to person, through which, therefore, fellowship between persons is created, it is through His Word that God realizes His will in and for man. Only the Word can put God's will before man in such a way that He is acknowledged as Person, and that man can 'react' to it, can answer it in a personal way — that is to say, in the way of decision. That God wills to have fellowship with man, to have man as an independent 'other' who is yet wholly dependent on Him, is manifest because God acts with man and upon man through the Word. Seen from the formal side, the Word is thus the center of the Biblical revelation, as 'the Son of Love' in whom God gives Himself to man is the same center in material respect. Therefore, the Son is the Word and the Word, the Son.

What is analogous to the divine Word in man as the second member in the relation of personal correspondence? At first we might expect a concept such as that of hearing or perceiving as corresponding in man to the divine Word in God. This is, indeed, the case in the Old Testament. Since we are concerned with a correlative personal act, however, there should be more than a mere passive acceptance on the part of man. Mere acceptance would be that mirrorlike subjectivity which can find place in relation to an object, but not between person and person. If what is said about personal correspondence as the fundamental category of the Biblical revelation is to be correct, a responsible act of man must be the response to the Word of God — an act in which the whole person is summoned and responds in order to receive the self-giving of God — a high, personal activity, the essence of which is this receiving. In the Bible, particularly in the New Testament, this act is called obedience-in-trust [*Vertrauensgehorsam*], *pistis*. The German word *Glaube*, connected in its original meaning with fidelity (loyalty) and love, has undergone such a shift in meaning that today it can hardly be used any more for a translation of the New Testament *pistis*, unless through interpretation it is defended ever and again from the fatal intellectualistic misunderstanding into which it otherwise will necessarily fall.

Pistis, obedience-in-trust, is the personal answer of self-giving to the Word of God. In this response of self-giving the divine self-communication first reaches its goal, and actual fellowship between God and man originates. In this two-sided yet unequivocal relation God is completely and wholly the Giver, the first, and man is completely and wholly the receiver, the second. In *pistis* is contained the personal acknowledgment of the Lord as Lord, obedience, and the personal acceptance of the divine self-giving love in grateful responding love. Faith is the complete self-giving of man which is consequent upon having received the unconditional self-giving of God. Faith is the single ' answering ' acceptance of the Word of God, the correct, fitting answer to the first freely given Creator-Word of God.

In the New Testament a rivalry (so to say) obtains between the two concepts *agape* and *pistis* as the designation for this divine activity being answered by human behavior. Why was not simply *agape*, the ' love in the sense in which the Bible speaks of love,' retained as the correct designation? While the Synoptic Gospels, and in a certain sense also the Johannine writings, in their connection with the Old Testament give the concept of *agape* pre-eminence over the concept of *pistis*, Paul — admittedly without this polemic and also without simply displacing the concept of love to God — moved the concept of *pistis* into first place. The answer to the question why he did this can be read only between the lines: the word *pistis*, obedience-in-trust, expresses more clearly than *agape* the dependence of the human act upon a foregoing divine act. *Agape* denotes *God's* act, the voluntary self-giving; *pistis* denotes, as something entirely and personally active, the receiving of this self-giving love, which admittedly as recipient of the divine love leads again to love. Paul thus wishes to say: Only on the ground of receiving the divine love, on the basis of *pistis*, can man love in the sense of *agape*, and this, man's love, is then no other than divine love. It can be called *agape* only in so far as it is actually divine love with which man loves God and his neighbor. Human *agape* grows out of the *agape* of God by virtue of *pistis*, by means of which man receives the divine *agape*. It therefore becomes clear only in the concept of *pistis* that the correct human response is the answer to God's action toward man. What we have named the relation of personal correspondence thus first becomes fully clear in the correlation between W*ord of God and* '*faith.*' In this pair of concepts the Biblical understanding of the relation between God and man and therewith also the Biblical understanding of God and man comes to a complete expression. God is the God who approaches man because He wills to be known only in His Word; and man is the man who comes from God because only in 'faith' has he his true being.

The Nature of Personal Correspondence Between God and Man. On the basis of what has just been worked out let us again consider the nature of this personal correspondence. Man trusts and believes the God who reveals Himself in His Word as Lord and as Love. By this is not meant that man could also come together in this trust with another god or another person, as if the activity indicated in the word ' faith ' were a general possibility, which only this time becomes actual face to face with God, which another time might be realized with anyone. The meaning rather is: even as God the Lord is not ' any ' Lord but is *the* Lord, namely, the unconditional sovereign, the Creator-Lord; and even as God's love is not ' any ' love, but is *the* love, namely, the unconditional or voluntary self-giving love, so also ' faith,' *pistis*, is not ' any ' obedience-in-trust, but *the* unconditional trust and *the* unconditional obedience. Therefore Paul can use *pistis* often in an absolute sense, without an object and without more precise qualification; he means ' *pistis* simply,' not any kind of *pistis* in a relative and otherwise used sense of the word.

This unconditional trust, this unconditional obedience-in-trust, is only possible where man meets unconditional sovereign power which at the same time is also unconditional love. To feel such trust toward every other person is not only not permitted but is not even possible: the phenomenologists would say ' essentially impossible.' *Pistis* in the New Testament sense is that total self-giving, that complete renunciation of one's own security, that utter dependence, which is only possible face to face with one whose being and acts are such that face to face with him one *can* afford to renounce his own security. Man stays concealed in his secure hiding place, secreted behind the walls of his I-castle; and nothing can really entice him out until one meets him who overcomes all the mistrust and anxiety about his very existence which drives him into self-security and there imprisons him. Man remains imprisoned within himself until the one meets him who can free him, who can break down his system of defenses, so that he can surrender himself, and in this surrender of self receive what he needs to enable him to abandon his securities; that is to say, until that one comes who gives man the life for which he was created. Only unconditional love, which brings man to self-fulfillment, and therewith gives him true selfhood and eternal life, can call out in him complete, unconditional trust.

The same holds for obedience, which together with trust forms a unity in ' faith.' Man can obey, in freedom, only Him who has an unconditional right to this obedience: the Creator-Lord. But no command can compel this obedience, since enforced obedience is not real obedience. Real obedience is freely willed obedience: but this means an obedience fulfilled without the mental reservation, ' How will I make out with this? ' — hence an obedience which is given immediately with unconditional trust, in which he who obeys knows that he will not be a loser. For this reason only *the* Lord, who at the same time is voluntary, self-giving love, can find such obedience. As holiness and mercy are one in the nature of God, as the will of unconditional self-affirmation ' over against ' the creature and the will of unconditional self-giving to the creature are also one in His nature, so in ' faith ' obedience and trust are one, but only in that faith which does full justice to this God, and which by means of His self-revelation is called into being by Him.

Faith as Dependence and Freedom. This 'faith' — awakened through God's love — is also the only possible union of complete freedom and complete dependence. It is the most personal of the personal. In it the person is present wholly and without reserve; the ' I ' ventures to come out of its shell and in so doing takes over the entire responsibility for its acts. In contrast with this trust everything else that man does is something partial, something which he cannot do ' with the whole heart.' For everything else that man does is conditioned: this alone is unconditioned. All else can satisfy only ' one side of him ': the whole man can only be satisfied when he himself becomes whole. Only in this way does he ' come completely out of himself,' with entire spontaneity, without stipulations and reassurance. Only here is he entirely himself — ' all there,' so to say — for nothing else is big enough to enable him to achieve a complete personality, even though he may perhaps be striving to achieve it or affirm it. Consequently only this faith is complete freedom.

On the other hand, only this faith is complete dependence. For it is release from the self, from what the self has, can do, or has done; release from glory in self and worry about self. Faith means that man places himself completely into the hand of God: and even more, that he takes himself completely out of the hand of God. In everything else that man does he holds himself back (so to say), he has a reserve, an

73

if and but: he remains his own free lord. In this action man gives up his right of self-determination and places himself entirely into God's hand for disposal. Even more: he not only thus places himself for disposal, but knows and acknowledges himself as one who has been disposed of from eternity. This is the secret of election, which is faith's profundity. Of it something will be said later. Faith means that one lives his life as that which has been wholly given to him, and thereby knows that in this way he first is really himself.

If we now ask what has been the result of this inquiry into the understanding of truth with reference to gaining insight into the Object-Subject antithesis (determined by the rational, ordinary conception of truth), our answer can be only a preliminary hint which will first be developed more exactly in the following chapter. If we ask what sort of truth man possesses in faith, what sort of truth he discerns in faith in God's self-revelation through His Word, it is as if with this question we had moved first of all into an entirely foreign context. In faith man possesses no truth except God's, and his possession is not of the kind whereby one ordinarily possesses a truth, but personal fellowship. We are beginning to suspect why in the Bible the word ' truth ' appears in what is for us a strange context with the words ' doing ' and ' becoming.' Faith, which appropriates God's self-revelation in His Word, is an event, an act, and that a two-sided act — an act of God and an act of man. *An encounter takes place between God and man.* While God is coming to meet man He also makes possible man's going to meet Him.

Overcoming the Object-Subject Antithesis. There is no longer a place here for the Objective-Subjective antithesis. The application of this pair of concepts in this connection is entirely meaningless. The self-revelation of God is no object, but wholly the doing and self-giving of a subject — or, better expressed, a Person. A Person who is revealing Himself, a Person who demands and offers Lordship and fellowship with Himself, is the most radical antithesis to everything that could be called object or objective. Likewise, the personal act of trust is something quite other than subjectivity — that subjectivity which can become actual only when it is over against an object, that subjectivity which appropriates what is foreign to it. If we were to speak of appropriation in this context, it could be only of such a kind as when man gives himself to God to be owned by Him. But if we know as believers we recognize what is meant here, that that which happens in revelation and faith cannot be pushed into the framework of truth and knowledge of truth without its becoming in that way something quite different. Yet in the Bible what we have been talking about is just what is called truth. ' I am the truth.' This Biblical ' truth ' is as different from what otherwise is called truth as this personal encounter and the double-sided self-giving and its resulting fellowship are different from the comprehension of facts by means of reasoning. This is not to say that there do not also exist between both this Biblical and the general rational conception of truth positive relations outside of these differences; this question is to be discussed in the following chapters. Our first result is this: the concern of the Bible is personal correspondence as it is realized in the correlation between the Word of God and faith; and, contrariwise, such an understanding of the concept of the Word of God and faith as is yielded by reflection about the fundamental Biblical category of personal correspondence. Through it the Biblical conception of truth is determined, and differentiated from every other understanding of truth.

The Origin of Man. In conclusion one further question might be answered, a question which in the course of our inquiry would necessarily arise without having gone into it any farther: of what kind of man have we been speaking thus far? Where is the man who answers God (as we have here supposed) while he obeys and trusts Him? Manifestly we have not spoken here of actual man, otherwise our speaking would have had to be about sin. Hence we have executed a thoroughly necessary abstraction. The concept of faith is more fundamental than the concept of sin; for sin is apostasy from faith, in which and to which man is called through creation. We need not presuppose sin to speak about faith; but we must presuppose faith to talk about sin. Not sin but faith is inherent to the created nature of man. In order to understand man and the man who comes from God we must be concerned, not with sin, but with faith. And we must, in order to understand what sin is, start our inquiry from man's 'original position' from which he through sin has fallen and is continuously falling. In this connection the sentence holds: *verum est judex sui et falsi* — truth is judge of itself and of the false.

The actual man is the one whose existence is determined by this falling away from his original position, from his divine origin. How the problem of truth, as the Bible speaks of truth, is represented with regard to sinful man who is called to faith through Jesus Christ is the subject of the next chapter.

CHAPTER THREE

··

The Biblical Conception of Truth
and Faith in Justification

··

CHAPTER THREE

The Biblical Conception of Truth and Faith in Justification

The thesis of our first chapter was that the Biblical understanding of truth is of a different kind from the general understanding of truth as determined by the Object-Subject antithesis. In the second chapter this thesis was clarified and proved, in a preliminary way, through the development of the fundamental Biblical category of personal correspondence, which lies at the heart of the Biblical conception of truth. The task of the present chapter is twofold: further to clarify and prove this thesis by testing it with reference to a specified part of the Biblical proclamation — faith in the justification of the sinner; and to elucidate in such a way that not only it but also this core of the Biblical message is thereby clarified. Since we are concerned with a problem which on the one side is also the subject of philosophy, a brief consideration of the relation between our inquiry and a philosophical inquiry is necessary.

The Object-Subject Antithesis in Thinking. The antithesis or the correlation of object and subject has dominated all Western philosophy since its very beginning. Being and thinking, truth and knowledge — this is the problem around which philosophical thought has turned at least since the Sophists and Socrates — a problem that emerges again in Kant's question about the relation between the 'thing-in-itself' and experience. The ultimate validity of this way of stating the problem has not been questioned until very recently. One did not ask if the truth could be found by means of these methods of reasoning, but merely which of the two great categories, the Objective or the Subjective, should be considered primary and what sort of relation obtained between the two. On this issue the great systematic trends of thought separated, Realism with its primary emphasis upon the object, Idealism with its primary emphasis upon the subject, Pantheism or the Doctrine of Identity with its tendency to make the antithesis a matter of indifference. It was left for the newest form of philosophy, the existential, to question the validity of the antithesis itself. It is no accident that the source of this new thinking is to be found in the greatest Christian thinker of modern times, Sören Kierkegaard. It is therefore particularly suggestive for us theologians to attach ourselves to this philosophy, the entire bent of which seems to correspond with ours. Yet we must emphasize again that our considerations are purely theological, that hence they are not dependent upon the correctness or incorrectness of that philosophical undertaking which seems to run parallel — apparently or really — with our own. There are no preliminary philosophical judgments which we carry over to be added to theology; we are concerned rather with something *sui generis*, namely, the correlation between the Word of God and faith. The nature of this relation cannot be derived from any general philosophical propositions — were they even those of existential philosophy — but must be understood on the basis of primary knowledge of that correlation itself, as only faith can have such knowledge. It is only the *false* subordination of the correlation Word-of-God/faith under the Object-Subject antithesis and the concept of truth determined by the antithesis — hence not what is essential but a *misunderstanding* — which is necessitating us when we make use of this general philosophical terminology.

At first it seems indeed to be a completely impossible undertaking to wish to withdraw oneself from between this pair of tongs (as it were) of the two concepts Objective-Subjective. They seem to be so necessarily linked with the process of thought as such that theological thinking too, it would seem, could not be done without them. As soon as one thinks at all, how can one help thinking ' something,' how help wanting to think what is objectively true? But we would thus concede that all thinking, including theological, takes place within this antithesis and is unable to proceed outside it. The theologian too when he thinks places the truth over against the false meaning; it therefore seems wholly senseless — yes, even bootless — to wish to attack this fundamental law of all thinking.

Indeed for theology as the science of faith, as systematic reflection about faith in its relation to the Word of God, this law is valid. But the theologian is concerned, not with theology, but with the Word of God and faith. For the theologian this correlation Word-of-God/faith is the ' subject ' which he represents, which he portrays as ' objectively ' as possible — this must be understood first of all, although at once it must

be more closely qualified and delimited. As thinker he suc-
cumbs, like every other thinker, to that fundamental relation
of all thinking; he remains between the tongs (so to say) of
the Object-Subject antithesis. But that *which* he is to comprehend is a ' subject' *sui generis;* that with which he deals
when he speaks about the Word of God and faith is precisely
not thinking but a discerning of truth of an entirely singular
nature. He should exhibit in its peculiarity what lies beyond
the Object-Subject antithesis, the encounter between the self-
revealing God and the man who, because of this revelation
of God, surrenders himself. Hence his ' subject ' — not his
thinking about it — lies beyond what can be comprehended
by means of the Object-Subject correlation. But not only this
— and now follows the qualification and more precise delimitation of the concession granted at first: he cannot perceive
this ' subject' in a purely scientific way, but only if he himself becomes a believer: that is to say, only if he withdraws
himself from the Object-Subject antithesis and meets in faith
the God who meets him in the Word. This doubleness —
that on the one hand he is a scientific thinker, comprehending
objectively, and on the other a believer — is the particular
burden and difficulty of theology. The theologian is really a
wanderer between two worlds.

Resolution in Faith of the Object-Subject Antithesis. In
thinking the Object-Subject antithesis is present. But in faith
thinking is precisely what does not concern one. What is
constitutive in thinking, that *I* think *something* — this distinguishing between the objective and subjective — finds no

place in faith, if our understanding of faith (as it has been to this point) has the closest possible connection to the Pauline usage of the term. Of course there is also the colloquial way of speaking, ' I believe *something* '; but at this point we give up the position we maintained when we spoke of the true Biblical faith; we give up the position of personal correspondence. In dealing with genuine, primary faith, i.e., when God reveals Himself to me in His Word, we are not then concerned with a ' something.' In His Word, God does not deliver to me a course of lectures in dogmatic theology, He does not submit to me or interpret for me the content of a confession of faith, but He makes Himself accessible to me. And likewise in faith I do not think, but God leads me to think; He does not communicate ' something ' to me, but ' Himself.' The counterpart is no longer as in thinking a something, a something pondered and discussed which I infer through the energy of my thinking, but a Person who Himself speaks and discloses Himself, who Himself thus has the initiative and guidance and takes over the role (so to say) which in thinking I have myself. An exchange hence takes place here which is wholly without analogy in the sphere of thinking. The sole analogy is in the encounter between human beings, the meeting of person with person.

From this analogy are taken the conceptual means of expression with which we can represent in words what takes place between God and the man who has faith in the Word. Yet we are dealing *only* with an analogy seen in an exception to the usual occurrence, and we will speak about it immediately. The encounter between two human beings is ordinarily not personal at all but more or less impersonal. I see 'someone.' To see some*one* is not essentially different from seeing some*thing*. This someone says something to me. Someone saying 'something' to me is not essentially different from my saying 'something' to myself — that is, thinking. But now let us put the case that this someone does not say 'something' but 'says' himself, discloses himself to me, and that I, while he 'says' himself to me, 'hear himself'; and more, that while he discloses himself to me, and so surrenders himself to me, I disclose myself to him and receive him, while I surrender myself to him. In this moment he ceases to be for me a 'someone-something' and becomes a 'Thou.' In that moment in which he becomes a 'Thou' he ceases to be an object of my thinking and transforms the Object-Subject relation into a relation of personal correspondence: we have fellowship together.

Provided that this occurs in ordinary experience, the difference between the 'something-someone,' my object and the 'Thou,' is, to be sure, relative, not absolute; the line of demarcation is not sharp — rather, the actual experience always has a mixed character. Consequently, this personal encounter and this fellowship are only analogous to what takes place between God and myself in the relation of revelation and faith. But this relative analogy can guide us even in what in faith is meant, not relatively, but unconditionally. We understand that when God speaks with me the relation to a 'something' stops in an unconditional sense, not simply in a conditional sense as in an ordinary human encounter. When I stand opposite to God, I am face to face with Him who unconditionally is no 'something,' who in the unconditional sense is pure 'Thou.' Therefore I have nothing to 'think'; that is to say, I have nothing spontaneously to disclose. He alone is Discloser. In this relation of facing one another, not only that 'which' is opposite becomes something other — a Thou instead of a something — but the entire relation undergoes a fundamental change, and that in the following way.

When I perceive 'something,' this 'something' is then within me; it becomes, so to say, my possession. I embrace it. In knowing it, I dispose of it. That which is perceived, that which is known, is at my disposal. The other side of this process is that I myself am not actually affected by it. My knowledge certainly enriches me; it may also have influence in my decisions, on my way of thinking; but it never penetrates to the core of my person — it does not transform 'myself.' I am, after all, the one embracing; I am the possessor.

A third point is to be noted. This knowledge unquestionably enriches me, it broadens my horizon; but it does not lead me out of my I-orbit, it leaves me solitary. This is also true if the object of my knowledge is human beings and if my knowledge about them is deeply searching: even then, since I know only about them, I remain solitary. Yes, even if these persons are not only known, but if they approach me, if they enter into relations with me, speak with me, if they in a relative sense thus encounter me and become 'Thou' — even then I remain solitary until one of these persons does not merely say 'something' and give 'something' but discloses himself and so gives himself to me.

Knowing, thinking, possessing something is thus, first of

all, something over which I have disposal; secondly, something that does not essentially change me; and, thirdly, something that leaves me solitary. But if the Word of God meets me in faith, this is all reversed. Then I do not have something like property which is at my disposal, but I myself become property; then I myself become disposable. This is what faith stammeringly says in the word, 'My Lord.' Faith says it, indeed, with the words denoting 'having something,' with the possessive pronoun 'my' — for our speech is formed out of our everyday life, out of that life where we possess; and yet this 'my' means exactly the opposite, not that God stands at my disposal, but I at His. Herewith, in the second place, a radical reversal occurs. Faith is no longer like that knowing which enriches, which leaves me unaltered in the core of my person; on the contrary, it precisely does not give me 'something,' but does change me in the very core of my person. Out of a lord faith converts me into a servant, and therefore transforms the whole meaning of my existence. The 'content' of my person, indeed, is left how and where it is, but the ruling principle is changed; much as if a man buys a house from another and does not alter the house but executes a 'change of hands.' That is faith: a change of hands, a revolution, an overthrow of government. A lord of self becomes one who obeys. And, thirdly, solitariness is now also past. The imperious, reserved I is broken open; into my world, in which I was alone — alone too in spite of all my 'something' and my 'something-someone' — into the solitariness of the 'Thou-less' I, God has stepped as Thou. He who believes is never solitary. Faith is the radical overcoming of the I-solitariness. The monologue of existence — even that existence in which many things have been talked about with many people — has become the dialogue of existence: now there is unconditional fellowship.

That God in His Word does not speak 'something' but Himself also changes the way of 'speaking.' God Himself speaks to myself: that is to say, His speaking is address. Previously we expressed it in this way: God delivers to us no course of lectures in dogmatic theology; He submits and explains to us no confession of faith. He does say to me, 'I am the Lord, thy God.' His Word is claim and promise, gift and demand. Likewise 'knowing' also acquires a new meaning. No longer is it a question of the insertion of something into the knowledge I possess, the expansion of the intellectual riches at my disposal; but it is answering personally when personally addressed, and hence obedient, thankful confession and prayer. Here as above the third person is replaced by the second person. 'I am the Lord, thy God' bespeaks the answer, 'Yes, I am Thy obedient servant and Thy child.'' The true form of faith is hence not the so-called declaration of faith, the formulated Credo which has been learned, but prayer; even as the Word of God is not a formulated 'to the believer,' but challenging, freely given address. The antithesis between Object and Subject, between 'something truthful' and 'knowledge of this truth' has disappeared and has been replaced by the purely personal meeting between the accosting God and the answering man. It is only *reflection* about faith which explains this personal occurrence in the second person as an impersonal twofold set of facts in the third person:

Credo in the sense of being directed toward the believer, credo in the sense of being accepted by the believer. Between the Word of God and the obedience of faith on the one hand and Credo-credo on the other lies an abyss, namely, the abyss that lies between the Biblical and the general, rational understanding of truth.

Agape. A short time ago we said that intercourse between human beings is an analogy — but no more — to what takes place between the Word of God and faith, with the exception of one instance where the analogy becomes identity. This instance in human relations which is not only analogy but the thing itself is called *agape* in the Bible. The ordinary personal relation between persons is intermediate between the personal and the nonpersonal. In other words, the ' natural man ' knows the difference between person and thing, between ' Thou ' and ' It,' only in a relative sense. Of course conceptually we distinguish readily enough between an encounter with a person where the concern was only about ' something' and an encounter where we met as ' I ' and ' Thou,' in which we disclosed ourselves to each other and so had fellowship together. And yet at the same time this ' Thou ' is for us always someone who is talked about in the third person, from whom we want something or whom we in some way would like to incorporate into our I-estate. What is lacking is the radical overcoming of the ' I-It ' relation by the ' I-Thou ' relation; what is missing is the radical relation of love. The ' I ' — as sinner, let us say now in anticipation — always confronts the ' Thou ' in a dominating and possessive relation which does not permit true fellowship to develop. The Bible tells us that overcoming the lack of fellowship between men in any event cannot be accomplished by us, that rather it can be accomplished only when man through the Word of God in faith has fellowship with God. When this faith actually comes into being, that change in the relation to men also takes place: the *agape* of God becomes determinative also for the relationship among men. For ' faith,' *pistis*, is efficacious in ' *agape* '; only such a faith, says Paul, is meant and only such love is really *agape*. But this does not happen when faith has the form of Credo-credo, that is to say, where the Thou-form of the occurrence has been translated into the It-form of reflection; it happens only when faith is a personal answer to the personal Word of God. This faith proves itself at once and necessarily in *agape*, while the other (as we theologians know particularly well) can be present very well with a complete want of *agape*.

The Word of God and Doctrine. For the present we have aspired to nothing more than elaborating clearly the abysmal difference between personal faith, as we know it from the fundamental Biblical category of personal correspondence, and a Credo-credo faith which originates in the transition from the second to the third person, from the personal to the nonpersonal relation. Because of the entire Church tradition and the Biblical usage of language, it is a matter of course that we must trace not only the antithesis but also the positive and necessary connection between these two very different conceptions of faith. For even if God does not deliver a course of lectures in dogmatic theology or submit a creed to us, but addresses us, so on the other hand it is not to be denied that in His Word God gives us Himself in no other way than that He says ' something ' to us. In other words, the Word of God contains doctrine in some way, and the faith which is the answer to prayer entails knowledge. It will, therefore, be necessary to reflect more precisely about the relation between the personal and nonpersonal elements. The time has not yet come, however, for this reflection; we shall have to substantiate the knowledge just won before we can turn to the second task, or else we run the danger of losing all that has been gained. In which relation faith is to be considered — in the primary, personal sense or in the secondary nonpersonal, in the sense of second or in the sense of third person, in the sense of answer to prayer or in the sense of acknowledging a doctrine — is manifestly a very important and yet secondary question which we will take up in the next chapter. First of all, something else is necessary. Instead of speaking in general, as we have been doing, about Word of God and faith, we wish now to penetrate to the center of the evangelical proclamation and examine what has been explained previously about *the* Word of God and *the* faith; explain what is related to our concrete situation, namely, that we are sinners.

The Word of God in Our Sinful Actuality: The Law. The Word of God meets us in our actuality, as sinful men. It tells us that we are sinners, that we live in contradiction to our God-given appointment, that we have denied our dependence on God (in which we are created) through our misuse of the freedom of choice given us. In this way we have lost the fellowship with God which becomes actual only when we acknowledge our dependence on Him. As sinners, we do not live without God, since God does not forsake us; but we live without fellowship with God, under His wrath. All of this is told us in the Scriptures, God's Word. Does, then, the Word of God after all tell me ' something about myself '? Does it somehow describe a set of facts just like knowledge in the sphere of natural knowledge? Does it, then, reveal to us, as would a mirror held before the eyes, that which is in us, and tell us therefore what we could see in ourselves if only we could see accurately? Is this really the Word of God?

Indubitably it is, in a certain sense. The Word of God, provided that it does this, is what Paul terms ' the law.' We shall be judged according to the creation-established norm of our being, by the standard of what we should be according to the appointment of the Creator, and this judgment is as follows: We have missed our destiny, have perverted our being, and therewith also have lost the life which was given us with our destiny. ' Through the law comes knowledge of sin.' Likewise, ' The law worketh wrath.' Both mean that the law reveals to us the opposition between the Will of God and our being. The knowledge given us by the law does not disclose anything new about our being, but only makes apparent this being. With this set of facts the other as substantiated by Paul agrees, namely, that knowledge of the law is of such a nature that man could develop it out of himself — that indeed, in a measure and to a certain extent, he does develop it out of himself. The law is written in his heart, and the bad conscience is a sign of its efficacy.

For this reason the law is not the Word of God in the real sense. As Paul shows us in Galatians, it is preliminary and mediating; it has ' come in between.' God meets us in it, and yet He does not meet us as Himself. Hence no fellowship with God originates in the law; nothing new is created, but what is already in existence comes to be known. Paul says something even more daring about the law: it causes sin itself, although in substance it is divine. It is that kind of knowledge of God which is linked with our being sinners. The legalistic understanding of God's Will makes us independent of God in a false way — in a way which corresponds to sin. It awakens the delusion in us — not by chance but necessarily — that we can do God's Will by ourselves, if we only want to; it seduces us to self-righteousness and self-glorification. In the light of the law we falsely understand — we sinners — God-given autonomy as independence from God; we think ourselves self-sufficient and self-existent. The legalistic understanding of God and our relation to Him is therefore as false as sin itself; indeed Legalism is actually the very heart of sin.

God's Act of Atonement Apart from the Law. When Paul begins to speak of the true Word of God after he has described the actual condition of man under the law, he inserts the words: ' But now the righteousness of God, apart from the law, is revealed.' He then discusses God's act of atonement in Jesus Christ and the freely given righteousness of faith stemming from freely bestowed grace. Faith is not concerned

94

with the law but only with the Word of God. With faith in this Word the legal relation between God and man comes to an end. In this Word man receives the new life; he becomes a new man. Of this Word alone it can be said that through it the love of God is poured out in our hearts and fellowship is established between God as Father and ourselves as His sons. We must hold to this conception of the Word of God if we would know what the Bible means by the Word of God in the real, strict sense.

God reveals Himself, we explained earlier, in the justification of the sinner — reveals Himself as Lord and unconditional Love: that is to say, He reveals His unconditional will to Lordship and His unconditional will to fellowship. Paul draws both together into one concept which is hardly comprehensible to the Gentile: *the righteousness of God.* The meaning of the phrase can be discussed under three headings.

First, in this manifestation God reveals His essential being. He is the first, the One who is unconditional, freely ruling, bound by no presuppositions, the Creator-Lord. What He pronounces, happens; His Word is not derivative, but creative. He pronounces justly upon sinners, as He is just. This being of man, this new being which stands in contradiction to the old, has its ground and continuance only in His spoken Word.

Secondly, in this revelation God expresses His real being as love given without necessity, love given unconditionally. That the divine love is given without necessity is nowhere proved so unmistakably as when He gives His love to one who has forfeited it, who has merited His anger. God loves His enemies. But that is not all: He loves even those who wantonly utilize the highest gift He has bestowed on them — freedom — to turn against Him. It thus becomes manifest that God's love is determined in no way by the worth or disposition of those loved, but absolutely by His willing to love them. His love is as freely given as it is unconditional. He gives it gratis, without any proviso except what is ineluctably part of giving, namely, that one accepts what is given. He gives love unconditionally to him who accepts it, which is to say, to him who believes.

Thirdly, while God is exercising His sovereign jurisdiction and His sovereign Creator-might, He is establishing at the same time unconditional fellowship. God is concerned about the revelation of His righteousness, about the manifestation of His majesty, His sovereignty; but while God expresses His Lordship, His unconditional sovereign honor — while He asserts Himself as the Lord God — He gives Himself to man at the same time in His Son, even while He takes on Himself the whole threatening wrath, the whole curse of sin, and while He so manifests His will by giving everything to those to whom He has given Himself in His Son. What does this mean in view of our question?

First of all, then, God in His Word of justification offers Himself to men: that is, He offers fellowship with Himself, and His very life. God does not merely say ' something '; but while he says ' something ' He ' says ' Himself, He manifests Himself, He gives Himself. A something no longer stands between God and man. This impersonal something was the law. Paul makes use here of the concept *gramma,* the letter. The task of the law is the task of the letter of the alphabet. The law is that which came between, an indirect-ness, an abstraction, something fixed, which undoubtedly in-dicates God's will, but in which God is not present as Himself. The law is ' a truth,' something objective which one can know without in that way becoming essentially changed, an idea about God's will in which one has nothing to do with Him as One immediately present. That which has come between is removed; God broke through the law as through the curse of sin with His Presence, in the highest degree personal.

The Relation of Personal Correspondence in Sonship to God. Over against *gramma* Paul sets *pneuma*, the Spirit. God is present in His Word; His Word is Spirit and life. God does not will to exist as Something, as Abstraction, as an ob-jective Given, as any Other; but rather as a personal, and therefore not a strange, Other, as One living within the hearts of believers, through the Holy Spirit testifying to Himself as Father within themselves. An incomprehensible exchange now takes place. The human *I* is dethroned and God sets Himself on the throne in man. The domineering *I* is ' de-posed ' by the ruling Spirit of God. The Spirit of God bears witness to our spirit, that we are children of God. Yea, the Spirit itself cries, ' Father.' The Spirit of God Himself prays in our prayers. The Father, who has come out of His mystery and near to us in His Son, bears witness to the Spirit as *our* Father: He tells us that *we* are God's children. Consequently it is God Himself who does everything, upon which doing and saying alone man's new being depends.

And yet here too the relation of personal correspondence is

not resolved, but is first rightly established. It is God's right-eousness, *sola gratia*; but it is at the same time the *righteous-ness of faith*. God speaks His Word and in His Word brings Himself into the presence of man; but the real Presence actu-ally comes first and only through faith, through that obedient trust and trusting obedience, that affirming in which man surrenders Himself to the God who has already given Himself to man, in which man accepts God's Word of love. For this reason Paul speaks as often and as emphatically of a righteous-ness of faith as of the righteousness of God. We said that the love of God is unconditional: it makes only the condition which lies within its nature, that man accept it. God does not force faith upon anyone. None comes to faith except through the act of repentance and the act of trust. 'Behold, I stand at the door and knock. *If any will open to Me,* I will go in with him and sup with him.' '*That whosoever believeth in Him* shall not perish.' '*To as many as received Him,* to them gave He power to become sons of God, *who believed on His name.*' The Lord has given the invitation: but the question arises whether the ones who have been invited will come.

Personal Correspondence in the Obedience of Faith. As clearly and unmistakably as the Bible teaches God's all-effi-ciency in which everything is grounded, so it impresses un-ceasingly and indubitably that the Word of God *furthers* the obedience of repentance and faith. It is of the utmost impor-tance to notice the particular passage in the Epistle to the Romans in which Paul first speaks of the Holy Spirit. It does not occur until the fifth chapter, after the discussion in the entire fourth chapter was about the obedience of faith. Through repentance and faith God imparts His Holy Spirit. Man, to whom the Word of Christ and the forgiveness of sins is preached, to whom God in His mercy offers Himself, is not admonished to wait until the Holy Spirit is also given him — as if he himself could do nothing at all. Rather, he is told that he should believe the Word which is told him. The human subject, the human person, is not blotted out, is not ignored, but on the contrary is called up, is summoned in the most urgent way: Be reconciled to God! Hear, believe, obey, repent, and have faith in the Lord Jesus Christ!

This personal correspondence — this paradox for our thinking as determined by the Object-Subject antithesis — is set aside in no Biblical passage, but ever and ever again is emphatically stressed as the high point of the proclamation of grace. God wills to have a counterpart who in free decision says 'yes' to Him. God does not overwhelm man, He does not annul the human will, the power of personal decision, but makes a claim upon it. God is Lord, He is not causality. God does not make Himself Lord in the manner of a superior force which overpowers what it meets, but He makes Himself Lord precisely by means of this claim for faith and claim for obedience — and never otherwise. This point should be emphatically stressed because it is just in this area that time and again a non-Biblical thinking has transformed the idea of God into a doctrine about an abstract absolute. In this way the understanding of the Biblical message has been obscured.

Nowhere in the Bible is it stated that it is God who believes the divine Word, as the false Objectivism attempts to maintain. In the Bible it is always man alone who believes, man alone who repents. But this faith of man, the affirmation of the Word of God, the acknowledgment of the Lordship of God in obedience, and the acceptance of the divine mercy in trust, is of such a nature that precisely in it man renounces his autocracy, thus relinquishing to the Spirit of God the throne of his I-lordship and giving up his place as lord of his life to God, the Lord. Beyond this the Bible never goes. For instance it does not go in the direction of the doctrine of the sole-efficiency of God. The doctrine of the sole-efficiency of God has a Neoplatonic, not a Biblical origin — even though it may have been defended by some of the most important teachers of the Church. It is therefore not Biblical, because it sacrifices the fundamental structure of the Biblical proclamation, the relation of personal correspondence, to a way of thinking which is determined by the Object-Subject antithesis.

The Realization of the New Life. But in one other respect we must beware of a false Objectivism. People have believed, supposedly in agreement with Luther but actually in contradiction to him, that one must understand the message of justification by faith alone in the sense of the later orthodox doctrine of forensic justification. This interpretation can in no way be blamed on Paul or, as has recently been shown, on Luther. The question involves the following: The Word of God promises us righteousness, it pronounces the sinner as righteous, which means as the one who is right with God, with whom God wills to have intercourse as with a son and no longer as with a rebel. This new status of the person — Paul calls it adoption into sonship — is grounded entirely in God's will and has its realization only in the Word of God. It is indeed as Luther said a 'strange righteousness.' 'Christ is my righteousness.' But the Bible, unlike many theologians, does not stop here. It goes farther and maintains that this righteousness actually becomes yours. God not only *declares*, He *creates* a new man. This new man is not only of a promised dimension, but one already realized if not yet perfected. So certainly as Christ, the living personal Word of God, does not *remain outside* ourselves but by faith *dwells* in us through the Holy Spirit, so certainly is the new man of no purely transcendent, eschatological dimension, but in faith is at the same time an experienced reality. We not only believe in the new man, but in faith we put him on, just as in repentance we not merely condemn the old man but actually put him off.

This realization of the new life is the content of the sixth chapter of the Epistle to the Romans. In faith the old man really dies; and in faith the new man actually lives. This is something quite different from maintaining that we merely believe that the old man is dead in Christ and that the new man lives in Christ. That is also true, but it is not the whole truth. Even while we believe that Christ died and rose for us, we actually participate in the dying and rising, and in this participation is our real new life. Thus here too personal correspondence is expressed in the Biblical proclamation. Christ *for* us corresponds to Christ *in* us; the righteousness *offered* us by God corresponds to the righteousness *accepted* in faith, which in being accepted comes to personal *actuality*. The new life is not only one in which we believe, but in faith it is real. Indeed faith itself is this new reality. Man in faith *is* the new man, life in faith *is* the new life.

How could it be otherwise? God's Word is always creative. His promise too, since it is laid hold of in faith, is a new birth. Through the Word of promise we are born again to a new hope. To be able to hope, the certainty of hope, is already in itself a new personal life. A believing and a hoping person is a different person — if he really believes, if he persists in faith, if, as the Johannine writings always express it, he ' abides in Him.' He who abides in God, in him God will also abide. Whoever abides not in God, in him God also will not abide. But whoever abides in Him obeys His commandments and does His Will. For the love of God is poured out in our hearts through the Holy Spirit. The ' love of God in our hearts ' is, according to Luther's word, *caritas*, with which the new man — in whom Christ through His Spirit is Master — meets God and his fellows. This love according to Biblical doctrine is not entirely in the future, but in believers is already of a realized dimension, even as the Holy Spirit, the pledge of the new life, is a present, creative reality in them.

Why is this so? Because in faith we are not dealing with a superior truth which remains over against us, but with the Word of God, by means of which God establishes fellowship with us. It is no accident that it was Orthodoxy — to be sure very early in the age of the Reformation — which defended the doctrine of the purely forensic nature of justification. The significant factor in Orthodoxy is that personal correspondence was crowded out by a conception of truth orientated about the Object-Subject antithesis. Orthodoxy thought of God as the teacher who delivered supernatural, revealed truth and proffered faith to man. In this way the Word of God was identified with doctrine, and faith was assent to this doctrine. Precisely that which is the concern of Biblical faith was consequently no longer understood: that is, overcoming the Object-Subject relation and having the real Person of God present in His Word, who as such is also the creative Presence of the Holy Spirit. For this reason the faith of Orthodoxy was so destitute of love. For love cannot be created by faith in a revealed truth, but only by the presence in the heart of the Holy Spirit, who is none other than the very love of God Himself poured out in our hearts. Faith in doctrine has never yet created new men: on the contrary, whenever it has usurped the place of true faith which is fellowship with God, it has always been singularly lacking in love. This is not surprising in the light of what we have come to understand. Whenever the highest place — the place belonging by right only to living faith — is given up by this faith to faith in doctrine, an abstraction, a truth, receives the highest distinction; and the relation to persons must of necessity remain subordinate.

The New Relation with Fellow Men. In conclusion, these considerations lead us back once more to the connection between the divine and human Thou-relation, which earlier we wished to comprehend only as analogy. We have already spoken of the one instance in which it becomes more than an analogy. If it is indeed true that through faith we have real fellowship with God, that hence in faith the new person, the new man comes to realization, then the new relation with fellow men is also thus determined. The old relation was characterized by the fact that in all fellowship the dominating attitude which has the I as its object crowded in. The 'Thou' was always at the same time someone, a subject for discussion, a third person, an object, and therewith at the same time 'something' with which I start something, over which in some way I take command. But the change that takes place with faith will also change this relation. While man places himself under the Lordship of God, while man has fellowship with God who is Love, his fellow is also face to face with him in a new way, no more as object but as 'Thou.' In faith we can regard our fellow man in no other way than that Christ meets us in him, Christ helping us. The human lordly I is dethroned by the I of divine love; hence faith is of such a nature that it proves itself efficacious in love. Through faith and through it alone our fellow man becomes, like God, an actual 'Thou.' For love, with which a man of faith meets his fellow, is after all not his, but 'the love of Christ constraineth him.' But while this love moves him, he has first become — or rather he has started to become — that for which he was created, a man who comes from God and goes to God.

CHAPTER FOUR

••

The Biblical Understanding
of Truth and Doctrine

••

CHAPTER FOUR

The Biblical Understanding
of Truth and Doctrine

The previous chapter can be summed up as follows: The relation of personal correspondence, which we found to be the basic category of Biblical thinking and placed in contradistinction to the general understanding of truth, has conclusively proved itself to be at the center of Biblical faith in a primary and decisive examination of justification by faith alone. Faith does not depend on ' something true ' — even though this truth were something spoken by God — but has to do with God Himself, how He reveals Himself to us in His Word, is present with us, addresses us, and furthers in us the response of obedience-in-trust. Conversely, it is with reference to knowledge of the fundamental Biblical category that the nature of revelation and faith, of justification of the sinner, has become more intelligible in its true Biblical sense and without being encumbered with the orthodox tradition. It will now be our task to carry on this examination and corresponding elucidation of the basic category and content of the Bible — the formal and the material — with reference to several other chief concepts of the Biblical proclamation.

The Positive Relation Between the Word of God and Doctrine. But first there is another problem to solve. Thus far we have elaborated only the negative relation between the Biblical and the general concept of truth, namely, the complete difference between the two. But we have already conceded, if only in passing, the one-sidedness of this interpretation. The relation between Word of God and doctrine cannot be fully stated by saying that they are ' completely different.' This is clearly indicated, not only by the whole history of the Church, but also — and more significantly — by the content of the Bible itself. Even though it is true, as we previously said, that all doctrine in the Bible means nothing else and points to nothing else than that God Himself addresses us in order that we ourselves may answer Him in faith, it must surely be conceded at the same time that this address and this response can take place only by virtue of Biblical *doctrine*. Between the Word of God and obedience-in-trust on the one hand and doctrine and faith in doctrine on the other there must thus obtain necessarily and not only accidentally a positive relation in addition to the negative one. Of what sort is it?

Even as we previously said that the Word of God is not doctrine, that God in His Word does not speak ' something true ' but Himself, so now we must further ask: Does He not speak Himself to us in such a way that He tells us ' something,' ' something true,' so that doctrine after all is also contained in His Word? And if until now we said that faith, *pistis*, is something different from recognition of a truth, namely, trustful and obedient surrender to God, who imparts Himself to us, so we must also further ask: Can this faith be consummated in any other way except that we believe

' something ' ' which ' God says to us? With this double query we neither shall nor may call in question what we have been pointing out: We continue to maintain that an abyss lies between what happens in the meeting between God and man in revelation and faith, what happens in this occurrence in the second person and everything that has the form of discussion about ' something true ' in the third person. The question is whether this abyss is not bridged after all, whether in the act of God's speaking and man's thus being enabled in faith to hear and think the positive relation between Word and doctrine is not already also established.

Jesus Christ Himself Is the Word. It is of the highest importance that Jesus Christ Himself, the One in whom God imparts Himself to us, is called ' the Word.' It is therefore He, this Person, who is really the Word. He Himself is the communication, the self-communication of God; it is He Himself in whom God proclaims and realizes His will to Lordship and His will to fellowship. The new point of view in the New Testament in contrast to the Old is that God proffers us His Word no longer only in the words of the prophets but in the Word become flesh. It thus becomes unmistakably clear that what God wills to give us cannot really be given in words, but only in manifestation: Jesus Christ, God Himself *in persona* is the real gift. The Word of God in its ultimate meaning is thus precisely not ' a word from God,' but God in person, God Himself speaking, Himself present, Immanuel. ' *I* am the Way, the Truth and the Life.' ' *I* am the Light of the World.' ' *I* am the Bread of

Life.' ' Come unto *Me*, all ye . . . and *I* will give you rest.'
The incarnation of the Word, the entrance of God into the
sphere of our life, the self-manifestation of God in His Son
— this is the real revelation, the basis for Lordship, and the
means of establishing fellowship. Words therefore are not
of ultimate consequence, not even divine words, but the
Word, which He Himself, Jesus Christ, is. Thus because
He Himself is the Word of God, all words have only an instrumental value. Neither the spoken words nor their conceptual content are the Word itself, but only its ' frame,'
the means of conveying it. As God in His Word wills to
direct not only our thinking but ' ourselves,' so in His Word
He wills to give ' Himself ' — that is, Jesus Christ.

*Doctrine as Token and Framework, Indissolubly Connected
with the Reality It Represents.* But this is only one side of
the matter. The other is that we cannot grasp this ' content,'
the reality itself, except within this framework. The tokens
are not accidental to but necessarily connected with the content; without doctrine the content is nonexistent for us. God
indubitably says ' something ' to us in order to be present as
Lord and as Father in the Son through the Spirit. Similarly
the direct address in its very simplest form — ' I am the Lord,
thy God ' — when conceptually comprehended, conceals doctrine, ' theology.' God, to be sure, does not deliver to us a
course of lectures in dogmatic theology or submit a confession
of faith to us, but He *instructs* us authentically about Himself.
He tells us authentically who He is and what He wills for us
and from us. And likewise that which is simplest and most

direct, i.e., immediate, personal answer to prayer, also has its abstract form: ' Our Father, who art in Heaven.' Consequently we can never separate the abstract framework from the personal Presence contained in it, although certainly we must differentiate them. We know that we can never have the one without the other, and we know at the same time that the whole point is to have the personal contained within the abstract framework. Doctrine is certainly related instrumentally to the Word of God as token and framework, serving in relation to the reality — actual personal fellowship with God; but doctrine is indissolubly connected with the reality it represents.

In this connection we may remind ourselves of the Sacraments. As God Himself is present with us in the bread and wine of the Lord's Supper, in these tokens, so the Word of God wills to be present with us in words. This elucidating reference to the Sacrament is instructive in two ways. On the one hand, the Sacrament as the *verbum visibile* teaches us that the reality itself is not identical with the words, nor by any means fully represented in them. Especially while taking part in the Sacrament, we see and are given the signified reality, and thus are freed from an idolatry of words; our Lord instituted it precisely to show us that what is of moment is He Himself, not doctrine about Him. In order to be present with us He Himself can utilize in a sovereign way this *verbum visible*, which is not exactly language in the ordinary meaning of the word. On the other hand, it becomes clear in the Sacrament that the token is indissolubly connected with the reality signified. Our Lord wills to be present with us, not ' behind ' or ' beside ' but ' in, with, and under ' the token of the Sacrament. The idolatry of the token is error on the side of magic, the ' cursed idolatry,' as it is called in the Heidelberg Catechism; the separation of token from the reality signified is the error of the ' sacramentarian,' against whom Luther rightly fought. What is of moment is that our Lord Himself is present; but He is present only ' in, with, and under ' the token, be it doctrine or Sacrament to which we refer.

The Limited Yet Indispensable Nature of the Concept of Truth Determined by the Object-Subject Antithesis. The question with respect to our central problem is: The concept of truth determined by the Object-Subject antithesis which deals with ' something true ' is indeed foreign to what is ultimately the concern of faith. The fact remains that in faith we are dealing, not with truths, not even with divinely revealed truths, but with God, with Jesus Christ, with the Holy Spirit. But, on the other hand, this conception of truth or the truth presumed in it is indispensable as instrument, as framework, as token of that which is the concern of faith. Faith, in other words, is in the final analysis not faith in something — something true, a doctrine; it is not ' thinking something,' but personal encounter, trust, obedience, and love; but this personal happening is indissolubly linked with conceptual content, with truth in the general sense of the word, truth as doctrine, knowledge as perception of facts. God gives Himself to us in no other way than that He says something to us, namely, the truth about Himself; and we cannot enter into fellowship with Him, we cannot give ourselves to Him in trustful obedience, otherwise than by believing 'what' He says to us. Since, therefore, this conjunction of token and reality, of signification and what is signified, is already given in the act of divine revelation, we call the connection not only instrumental but sacramental.

The Connection Between the Two Concepts of Truth. The connection between the two conceptions of truth has not yet been sufficiently clarified to avoid the possibility of deviating toward a false Objectivism or an equally false Subjectivism. In agreement with the whole Church we say that the Bible, the entire Holy Scriptures, is the Word of God. As in its totality it is event, so in its totality it is authority. But to this first assertion a second must at once be added. Not everything in the Scriptures stands in the same connection to the essential meaning. As I pointed out elsewhere with reference to the Church, so in the Bible it is true that there are differences between what is contiguously and what is more distantly connected to this essential meaning; there is *a connection more intimate or less intimate.* Carefully to note this difference is a matter of the highest importance; not to do so is a serious subversion to faith and the Church. There is nothing in the Bible that is not connected with what is its central concern; for everything after all is linked with the sequence of events in the history of revelation, with the truth content in the revelation of the living God who has conclusively made His Name known to us in Jesus Christ. But it is foolish to maintain that everything in the Bible — for example, detached bits of historical narrative — is connected in the same way to its essential content, to Jesus Christ, to the Word of God. There are, for example, the local references in the Gospels, which indeed are not inconsequential for a knowledge of Christ; for it is of the greatest importance that Jesus Christ lived and suffered, not just anywhere, but in specific places. And yet the local references considered singly are for the most part not of great importance, and not too much depends upon whether or not they are right. Similarly, Jesus Christ is not revealed to us otherwise than in the history of Jesus of Nazareth; but most of the single items of this history are not of the same decisive importance as the fact of His death on the cross. Likewise much in the letters of the Apostle Paul is indeed not inconsequential for an understanding of his message; and yet it would be absurd to maintain that the list of greetings in Rom., ch. 16 is as momentous — in the sense in which the Word of God is momentous — as for instance vs. 21–31 in the third chapter of the Epistle to the Romans. The Bible, figuratively speaking, is not a level plain, but a crater in which everything is orientated about one point. The nearer one is to this point, the nearer he is to what is quintessential. The Reformers suggested a similar difference when they separated the 'history' from the 'doctrine' — as, for instance, Luther with reference to the Christmas 'history.' The primary concern, he said, is not so much with the 'history' — by which he meant the self-evident, detached items — as with the 'doctrine' — by which he meant the actual occurrence of salvation and revelation, the Word becoming flesh. In 'doctrine' God tells us who He is and what He wants with us; hence through it we have fellowship with Him. Of course, this does not destroy the force of what was said at the beginning of the second chapter about history and doctrine, namely, that narrative and not doctrine is the adequate form to express the essential message of the Bible. This message is that 'narrative' which is caught in one sentence in the Fourth Gospel: 'The Word became flesh, and we beheld His glory.' In so far as the 'doctrine' in this Johannine word depicts this happening, it is immediately close to what is central, to what is essential in the Bible.

Similarly the Church in every age — although not always with the same energy and the same expert knowledge — differentiated between the chief articles of faith and other doctrines that also necessarily belong to faith, but with which the tendency to error was less dangerous than with the cardinal doctrines. It is not without danger to make such distinctions; but the danger is even greater if one does not make them. For then every believer would actually have to be a learned theologian in order to be saved. In every correct catechism such a selection is made on the basis of more or less understanding of what is central. Perhaps one would need to say that this selection could not be the same for every age, since the question is not one of working out a timeless system of 'central truths of faith,' but of fighting a war in which the areas of combat (so to say) are especially appointed for every age. The discussion of this question, however, would carry us too far afield. In any event it must be clear on what basis the selection is made and why it is legitimate: It has to do with the close connection to God's immediate address in Jesus Christ Himself. The more unmistakably a doctrine points to this connection, the more the 'something' which is said constrains the thoughts to turn from looking at 'something' to looking at 'Himself': the more, therefore, the testimony about God enables one to hear His address, so much more immediate is the something, the doctrine, connected with the primary concern of the Holy Scriptures.

God's Freedom in His Revelation. But this principle of contiguity, which is also the means of distinguishing between pure and corrupt doctrine, must be narrowed down at once to its specific value by means of its opposite: God can speak to us by means of a word, but its contiguity to what is essential could not be known by itself without taking into account that particular event of divine speaking. 'The Spirit bloweth where it listeth.' God, because He willed it so, has indeed bound Himself of His own free will, by means of His historical revelation, to this happening which we call the history of revelation and salvation, the witness of which we have in the Holy Scriptures. Even as He spoke, as the living God, with Moses and Isaiah, not with Buddha and Lao-tse, so He gives us His Word in the Bible and not in any other religious book of the East. At all events He binds us unconditionally to this book, because He binds us to this history. But it is His free will and His gift, whenever and wherever through the Holy Spirit He actually wills to reveal His revelatory Word, wherever and whenever through the Word of Scripture He Himself wills to speak to us. To be sure, it can happen that the whole Bible remains closed to a man until all at once the meaning of one word strikes him — a word which by all theological criteria we should least have expected to have such evocative power. Indeed we must go farther and say: God can, if He so wills, speak His Word to a man even through false doctrine and correspondingly find in a false Credo-credo the right echo of His Word. This is no license for careless teaching and preaching or for theological relativism; for *we* are restricted to His historical revelation as well as to the evidence of it and therewith also to the principle of contiguity and the separation indicated by it between pure and corrupt doctrine. But God is not thus restricted, and His freedom limits the validity of that principle of contiguity and in the last analysis of pure doctrine. Even the closest connection of doctrine to the Word itself, as it occurs perhaps in pithy sayings in the New Testament, therefore remains incommensurably God's own Word, in a free relation, ultimately determined only by God's will, even though for us this freedom does not exist.

A concluding word must be said about the relation between God's Word and doctrine, and here we will use to good advantage for our formal problem the knowledge gained in the preceding chapter about the antithesis between law and Gospel. Doctrine seen by itself, that is, separated from the Word of God as the event of encounter, stands in the closest relation to the law. The possibility certainly exists that in his faith a man stops dead with the law as such and does not attain personal, spirit-produced and spirit-filled obedience-in-trust. Not only ' can ' this occur; rather is this the great negative experience of the Church in all centuries.

In so far as this happens, doctrine — perhaps the doctrine laid down in the confession of the Church or in dogma or in the catechism — is for man nothing other than law. In his faith he is not dealing with God Himself but with something true from God, with true doctrine about God. He has been challenged in the name of God, appealed to by the authority of God and the Holy Scriptures to acknowledge something as true, without its being God Himself. For God, through the power of the Holy Spirit, transforms within man's heart this impersonal truth, this 'something true,' into personal fellowship with Himself — even though the man was unwilling to give himself to God in obedience-in-trust. The claim of faith — 'you must believe that as God's Word' — remains for him in that foreign and impersonal area in which the law is, as long as it is only law; and correspondingly his obedience in meeting this claim is opposite to dutiful obedience, which is the only possible way to confront the law.

Whatever the content of this doctrine may be — it may be even the doctrine of atonement through Jesus Christ and of justifying faith — so long as it is not God Himself who speaks with man and while speaking meets him in fellowship, so long as doctrine confronts him as something taught by Church or Bible 'which one must believe if he wants to be a Christian,' his relation to it remains legal and bears all the marks of Legalism. Even Jesus and the grace of God is then law — *gamma*, the letter. But that has not happened upon which everything — everything! — in true faith depends: that through the Holy Spirit Christ Himself dwells in him. The love of God has not been poured out in his heart through the Holy Spirit. He believes in the Holy Spirit — because the Scriptures speak about Him — but he has not received the Holy Spirit, the Holy Spirit has not taken up dwelling in him; the Holy Spirit does not motivate him like the children of God, does not guide him, does not make him joyous, does not make him free. He who believes solely in doctrine only knows that these are all activities of the Holy Spirit — that is, after all, what the Bible teaches — but these activities do not occur in him; for this 'letter' too, as well as every other, has no living strength.

This faith, as the Reformers repeatedly point out, is therefore dead, powerless, and wholly without worth. It is a deception, a facsimile of the true faith, a counterfeit bill which has exactly the same markings as a good one, but the signature, the certification, is lacking. This faith is not written in the heart by the hand of God, but only by the hand of the Church, by the hand of the apostles. This faith, begotten by permutation, which clings to dogma or to literalism in Biblical interpretation, which exchanges bare doctrine, even though it be Biblical doctrine — the formulated confession, the 'something true' — for the living Word of God, is a blight which lies over the whole history of the Church. It is no accident but a necessity, as we now know, that this faith in dogma takes its rise in the Church at the same time with moralistic Legalism. This 'Credo-credo faith' very early — manifestly already at the time when The Epistle of James was written as warning against it — usurped the place of genuine faith, paralyzed the Church, and perverted its will.

But as the law, even though it is done away with in Christ,

is a tutor to bring us unto Christ, a divine 'stronghold' (*phroura*), which 'directed men to Christ,' so also is this faith in dogma, this legalistic Bible-faith. Since God does not speak with us otherwise than as he 'says something' to us in order to communicate Himself, so a certain amount of doctrine must be present before living faith can come into being. Of course this can be an extraordinarily small amount. That jailer was changed in one night from a pagan into a believer. This conversion manifestly took place with a minimum of doctrine; the same obtained with those 'three thousand souls' who on Pentecost 'were added.' If He has once become the teacher, God requires few words in order to teach; and because He is the teacher, it requires under certain circumstances a very small measure of doctrine on the part of man. The relation between doctrine and Word of God, we said, is in the last analysis incommensurable. It must suffice to recognize that an abysmal difference, and yet at the same time a necessary connection, lies between the two. Doctrine alone without the presence of the Holy Spirit is law and betokens Legalism; but human boasting about the freedom of the spirit is egoistic enthusiasm. The Reformation insight remains valid: Word of Scripture and Word of Spirit, personal directness in doctrinal indirectness, even as Jesus Christ must fulfill the law in order to free us from it.

1. *The Doctrine of the Triune God.* Only now are we in a position to undertake an examination and clarification of our thesis with reference to the primary contents of the Biblical message; for we know now what each separate doctrine

means: Each points to God Himself in His will to Lordship and fellowship, and to God Himself in His act which creates this Lordship and this fellowship.

The doctrine of the Triune God expresses just such a content. To be sure, at first it might seem as if this doctrine were an instance contrary to our tenet, that the God of the Bible is always the God who approaches man, whereas the content of this doctrine is God as He is in Himself, whose nature it is to be self-sufficient, who being from everlasting to everlasting has created the world in time not because He had to but because He willed to, who hence cannot be thought to be (like the 'Godhead' of Pantheism) only in everlasting correlation with the world and man. Is this not precisely the meaning of the doctrine of the Trinity, that God, independent of the being of the creature, is in Himself the loving One, the self-communicating One, the One who speaks? Certainly this is the content: God, who in Himself is Father, Son, and Spirit, who hence did not first need the world and man in order to be Father, Son, and Spirit. But the relation of this perception to our thesis is, not of a contradictory, but of a corroborative nature.

For this is just the meaning of the mysterious doctrine of the Tripersonal God: God as He is by and in Himself, in His unfathomable mystery, is none other than He who has manifested Himself in His revelation in Jesus Christ as the Lord and as the loving Father. The doctrine of the Trinity, the doctrine of the everlasting love of the Father for the Son and of the Son for the Father through the Holy Spirit, attacks the notion that God as He is 'by Himself' is another than God as He is 'for us' in His revelation. 'If you ask who he is: He is called Jesus Christ, Lord God of Sabaoth and is no other God.' God is therefore through all eternity the loving One; He is in Himself the loving One; the being of the creature, which indeed is realized in time in the act of creation, is established through all eternity in His loving purpose, in the loving nature of God. He has loved us through all eternity and elected us in His Son who is Love, who therefore is named the first-born before all creatures. God wills — even when we think about Him as He is in Himself — to be known as no other than that One who meets us in Jesus Christ, His Son, as the God who approaches man, the God who would communicate Himself and who in His self-communication glorifies Himself. We should not speculate about a 'God-in-Himself' ['*Gott-an-Sich*'] as if He were some other than the God who reveals Himself in Jesus Christ as the loving Lord; but we should know that through all eternity He is this One and no other, the Father, the loving One who imparts Himself.

Consequently the doctrine of the Trinity, as Luther and Calvin stressed time and again, is more a delimiting and safeguarding doctrine than a Biblical kerygma. The Bible does not guide us to reflect about God as He is in Himself — the doctrine of the Trinity time and again misled theologians into unprofitable speculations; but it guides us to recognize the Father in the Son through the Holy Spirit as the One who has loved us in the Son through all eternity. It diverts us from unprofitable speculation about God as He is in Himself through reference to God's historical revelation, to the God who meets us in His Word and in His act, and declares only this about God as He is in Himself, that He is no other than the Being disclosed to us in the historical revelation.

2. *The Doctrine of Election.* Just as little do the Scriptures teach us about a secret *double decree of God*. Whenever they speak of the eternal decree of God, they proclaim the decree of election and nothing else. The doctrine of the double decree is not Scriptural, but a speculative enlargement of what is given in the Scriptures. Even the ninth chapter of the Epistle to the Romans, which so often is cited as the *locus classicus* of the doctrine of the double decree — that some are predestined through all eternity to everlasting life, others through all eternity to everlasting damnation — says nothing about it, but teaches the complete sovereignty and freedom of the divine compassion. God's compassionate love for us has no other ground than His free, unnecessitated love. The creature has no claims upon God, God owes him nothing, He after all is the creature's Lord. That He has compassion for him is due to His love given without necessity. This eternal election is the holy secret of faith. This is what God says to him whom He creates His child in Jesus Christ and to whom He therefore promises eternal life, while through this His Word of love calls faith into being in him. Consequently the eternal decree of God should always be spoken of only in correlation with faith. Those elected are the same as those who love God. Election and faith, election and love of God are correlative concepts in the Bible. To be elected and to be one in whom the love of God is poured out through

the Holy Spirit is one and the same thing. All speculations about election outside of this correlation — this personal correspondence — should be avoided, as the preacher Luther always stressed. We should not grant leeway to the desire for intellectual investigation for its own sake, which is all the time spinning out more and more detailed questions; and the raising of impertinent questions should be discontinued. You wish to know who God is and what He wills? Then cling to His revelation in Jesus Christ; then believe in Him. Do this and you will know yourself to be elected; do not do it and you are lost. But then there is also nothing more to say about the eternal decree of God; for from the point of view of faith only the Word of God deals with it.

This incongruity and incompleteness, so annoying to this desire for intellectual investigation for its own sake, is the distinguishing mark of all Biblical doctrine over the question. For this reason the Biblical doctrine of election is a pattern for what we have shown to be the basic structure of Biblical thinking in the concept of personal correspondence. The thought of the double predestination originates in overstepping the delimitations of this doctrine drawn in the Bible. It originates, considered essentially, in the non-Biblical thought of the sole-efficiency of God or of the absolute God. It is therefore a temptation which lies very close to everyone who once knows about election — a temptation which we should withstand. The thought of the eternal decree in the Bible is the same as the thought of the eternal consummation in the Kingdom of God. The Bible has nothing to say about a *Gloria Dei* which fulfills itself in the misery of the damned.

For the *Gloria Dei*, as we shall later show, is identical with the consummate praise of God by the creature.

The logically unsatisfying nature of this doctrine — in distinction from the system of complete logical equipoise in the doctrine of the double decree — is always the sign that the relation between God's grace and man's decision can never be logically determined. We have only the two possibilities: either the logically satisfying system of equipoise, satisfying the claims of thought, whereby either divine sovereignty or human freedom, and hence the reality of decision, is nullified; or the validating of both the divine sovereignty and the reality of the free decision, whereby the logically unsatisfying paradox takes its rise. The doctrine of the double predestination is not paradoxical — it is logically satisfying — but it sacrifices the reality of human decision to Determinism; that is, it evades the basic Biblical structure of personal correspondence, which from its point of view is a logical annoyance. That afterward — after the freedom of decision apparently is changed through this logical system of equipoise — we affirm that human decision is a reality notwithstanding in no way makes the system as such paradoxical, but merely affirms something which by definition is ruled out. The claim of freedom comes too late; the system is closed, there is no place for it. The logical conclusion ruled it out. Theological thinking has here become metaphysical. The Biblical idea of God, in the last analysis, is crowded out by the philosophical, speculative one. The system of truth has become master over the Biblical faith in the God who always, while calling to faith, furthers the power of decision. It is therefore important to note that a theologian like Calvin, because he is essentially proclaimer of the Biblical word and not essentially thinker, never preached the doctrine of the double predestination but only expounded it in theological polemical contexts. Surely he suspected that this doctrine is not the concern of the Biblical message but the product of speculative thinking.

As the Bible thus speaks of the eternal divine decree — namely, the decree of election — the close connection between God's will to Lordship and will to fellowship on the one hand and man's complete responsibility on the other becomes fully apparent. Man's responsibility is grounded precisely in his having been elected. It is precisely out of the Biblical doctrine of election that the Biblical ethic develops. On the side of man divine election corresponds to obedience-in-faith and love — one may indeed make the statement more pointedly in view of the Biblical meaning: The divine election of man corresponds to the human electing of God as Lord. One passage in I Corinthians illustrates this point. In the eighth chapter, where Paul speaks of knowledge, we read: ' Knowledge puffeth up, but love edifieth. If any man thinketh that he knoweth anything, he knoweth not yet as he ought to know; but if any man loveth God, the same is known by Him.' Being known by God is the same as being elected, and being elected corresponds, like the divine love, to man's love for God. Likewise we read in the *locus classicus* of the New Testament doctrine of election, Eph. 1:4: ' He chose us in Him — in Christ — before the foundation of the world, that we should be holy and without blemish before Him in love.' I know of no more complete expression of what I mean by the fundamental Biblical relation of personal correspondence than in these two passages.

3. *The Imago Dei.* From the *doctrine of creation* which we placed at the beginning of all our considerations, I should like in this connection to examine only the Biblical thought about the *creation of man in the likeness of God.* What our thesis expresses is actually applied at this point to the theme of Biblical doctrine. What is meant by the idea of the *Imago Dei* in the Holy Scriptures?

At all odds this is clear first of all: In man God created something special, one excellent creature above all others, whose distinctive feature is that in some sense he is similar to the Creator. To me it is quite probable that the Old Testament passages which deal with the image of God in man at first wanted to say nothing else than this: Man is different from other earthly creatures because of the divine likeness given him by God, the most apparent expression of which is his power to rule over the other creatures. Man is derivative person, even as God is original Person. But even when we are thinking in terms of the Old Testament we may not lift this idea out of the entire context of the Biblical revelation. That man is derivatively what God is originally is for believers in the Old Testament most important of all in this connection. God has a different relation to men from what He has to other creatures. The superior position of man in the hierarchical order of creatures as such, however, is not important just here. He has intercourse with man; He reveals His will to him and expects obedience and trust from him.

It is not that man as he is in himself bears God's likeness, but, rather, that man is designated for and called to a particular *relation* with God.

In the Old Testament what we have called the relation of personal correspondence stands out (if I may so express it) in bold relief. Certainly God is always first, the Creator, the Giver from whom man has received everything that he has and is. It is, after all, God who has created him in His own image, who has given him his especially distinctive being and appointment. God's covenant with the people of Israel is similarly a covenant of grace, as the covenant with Noah was already a covenant of grace, originating in God's mercy and sustained in unutterable patience despite all the unfaithfulness of man. But man's being a free person, face to face with God, is stressed in the Old Testament with extreme urgency. ' See, I have set before thee this day life and good, and death and evil. In that I command thee this day to love the Lord thy God, to walk in his ways, and to keep his commandments, that thou mayest live. . . . But if thine heart turn away so that thou wilt not hear, . . . I denounce unto you this day, that ye shall surely perish. . . . I have set before you life and death, blessing and cursing: therefore choose life, . . . that thou mayest love the Lord thy God, and that thou mayest obey his voice, and that thou mayest cleave unto him: for he is thy life ' (Deut. 30:15 seq.).

The grace of God is first; yet it is not forced on man, but submitted to him. He is not overwhelmed by it, but he is treated as one who can and should make free decisions. Grace must be accepted by man: The love of God, if it is actually to come to life for man, must be responded to with answering love; God's Word of compassion, the freely given Good, if it is really to become a blessing, must be heard and retained by man. God binds Himself to man while making man's salvation the concern of His almighty Will; but this binding requires the human response of man's binding himself to God. This is the divine conditional, the divine-human if, the fixed fundamental law of the God-man relation in the Old Testament. Undoubtedly man is sinner, he is unfaithful, he denies; but God is compassionate and forgives sin. However, this covenant is conditional, as Ps. 103 shows us: He is ' compassionate to those who sustain His covenant and remember His commandments, to do them.' God wills to have as His counterpart a person with the power of free decision who in love responds to His love. This is the connection in which the concept of man's being made in the image of God is to be understood.

Herewith a connection is also made with the use of this concept in the New Testament. There the concept of the *Imago Dei* undergoes a radical transformation. There are, indeed, passages where the exact likeness of God is spoken of in the Old Testament sense as the essential characteristic of man as such, of everyone who bears the human face. (Luther no doubt noted this double usage of language and differentiated between the one as the *similitudo publica* and the other as the *similitudo privata*.) But in the critical passages which deal with the exact likeness, the presupposition is that man has lost this divine image and that it must be and will be restored through Jesus Christ. The connection with the innate image of God is not, therefore, given up. The New Testament does not further explain how both have a relation to each other — that every man is created in the exact likeness of God, and yet that as sinner he has lost that image so that only through Jesus Christ it can be restored again. To arrive at an explanation of what happens between the impressing of the divine image and its being lost, we must make use of a process of 'extrapolation' (so to say). To say that man has lost the image of God indicates that one no longer understands what the Old Testament meant by the expression: being person in the sense that every man, whether sinner or not, whether believer or not, is person as differentiated from the subhuman creature; for *this* essence of being a person is certainly not lost. The New Testament rather means more precisely what we have won again, by the grace of God in Jesus Christ, fellowship with God, essential humanness. To *this* image we are restored through Christ.

With the *Imago Dei* concept a further transformation has taken place: From a concept expressing a static characteristic it has become a concept of relation. ' But we all, with unveiled face beholding as in a mirror the glory of the Lord, are transformed into the same image from glory to glory ' (II Cor. 3:18). Paul depicts here the relation between man and Christ as that between a source of light and a mirror, but with the modification that the mirror through the additional influence of the source of light gradually becomes an all-powerful reflector. The *Imago Dei* is no longer a human characteristic which God once for all impressed upon man at the time of his creation; rather, it is now something which originates in Christ and man actually being face to face, in the influence of His ' countenance,' He as archetype forming the man who in faith appropriates that influence.

In this way we can state — one might almost say with conceptual theological precision — what we mean by the relation of personal correspondence. God creates for Himself in Jesus Christ through the Spirit a personal counterpart, who gives back to Him in a personal act what he has first received, love and the praise of God's glory. Man first becomes — after as sinner he had ceased to be so — similar to God by means of the love of God given to him in Jesus Christ, poured out in his heart by the Holy Spirit, which now also shines out from him in a manner commensurable with the Word of faith which proves itself efficacious in love, and in fulfillment of the words: ' Let your light so shine before men, that they may see your good works and glorify your Father who is in Heaven.' We also think of the word in the Epistle to the Philippians: ' That ye may become blameless and harmless, children of God without blemish in the midst of a crooked and perverse generation, among whom *ye are seen as lights* in the world, *holding forth* the word of life.'

This Pauline *Imago*-concept embraces in a remarkable way the anticipatory grace of God, Source of all life and good, the effectualness of this grace through the Word of God, the personal presence of God in Jesus Christ, the pure susceptibility of the man in faith, and the free return of what has been received in reciprocal love. In two other important passages this new concept of the *Imago Dei* is brought into clearer connection with man's freedom or his power to make decisions. ' Put

on the new man, that after God hath been created in righteousness and holiness of truth ' (Eph. 4:24). ' You have put
on the new man, that is being renewed unto knowledge after
the image of him that created him ' (Col. 3:10). The spontaneity of man is not eliminated through the grace in Jesus
Christ, but it first rightly comes into its own. In relation to
the grace of God, man is not tree or stone, but responding subject, responsible person; and faith, as certainly as it is God's
gift, is man's original decision. For it is true faith, as the Old
and New Testaments reiterate, only when it is ' faith of the
heart,' that is, when the whole person affirms this faith with
his words, but especially with his actions.

There is hardly another concept in the New Testament
usage which is so appropriate as that of the *Imago Dei* for
expressing what is meant by the relation of personal correspondence:

God the Giver, in sovereign freedom, face to face with man;
man, who responds with derived freedom, face to face with
God;

God's ' yes ' to man — to man who as sinner lives in contradiction to God; man's ' yes ' to God which is called into being
by God's ' yes ' — is called into being but is not forced, re-
maining always man's own decision;

God's Word from which responsibility stems — which as
Word of grace first really makes responsible; man's responsible
decision, which God furthers and awaits, and which He at the
same time gives;

the love of God which without setting any conditions turns itself toward man — man in whom no condition for merit is fulfilled — the love, however, which, just because of its unconditional nature, awakens trust in man, so that he takes the risk of laying himself completely and without reserve into the hand of this loving God, being conquered by this love; man who henceforth is so conquered by God's love that he returns God's love in reciprocal love;

this is what the New Testament seeks to express in the idea of the image of God in man.

4. *The Doctrine of Sin.* In this connection we can briefly sum up the Biblical *doctrine of sin*. The Old, as the New, Testament recognizes no other concept of sin than the understanding of it as man's self-chosen alienation from God, the Creator and Giver of all life. In this concept of sin the face-to-face relation between God and man consequently is expressed with particular penetration. Sin presupposes, on the one hand, that originally and inextricably the human being is *God's* human being, that he is not only created by God but indissolubly bound to God, be it in life or death, in salvation or disaster, in love or in anger; on the other hand, that man is genuinely God's counterpart, endowed by God with the power of free decision and therefore fully responsible for what he does, especially for his alienation from God. The connection between the two sides of this concept must be pointed out more exactly.

Even in sin man remains bound to God. He is always sinner *before God*; he sins always against God, with reference to

God. Sin is always opposition to God, disobedience to Him to whom we belong. It is rebellion. Sin is always an actual relation to God — that is to say a negative one, a perverted relation to God. Sin is indeed ungodliness — not in the sense that man is free from God, but that he would like to be free from Him. The parable of the Wicked Husbandmen depicts this ungodliness with incomparable clarity. Tenants they are and tenants they remain, even if they play themselves off as lords a thousand times and refuse to pay the rent. And, indeed, fundamentally they know that they are only tenants, not lords, but they do not want to admit it. They turn away from God in order that they need not see Him; they kill His messengers, but in so doing they nevertheless have a bad conscience. Precisely for that reason they kill His messengers, because they have a bad conscience. But it is decidedly true that through sin the image of God in the heart of man becomes a caricature. 'Although they knew God, they glorified him not as God, neither gave thanks; but became vain in their reasonings.' Idolatry is the resultant of two components: the God-given knowledge about God and human sin, hence a knowledge about God and yet no recognition of God. Recognition of God one can have only in faith and obedience, not in sin. But wherever man turns himself to God he realizes, ' Against Thee only have I sinned.' How could man sin against God if he did not stand in an indissoluble relation to Him, if he knew nothing of Him?

As man remains bound to God even in sin, so sin is also the proof of his God-bestowed power to make decisions for himself. Nowhere in the Bible is God made responsible for sin. Even the strongest emphasis upon the omnipotence of God has its delimitation at this point which is never overstepped. It is not as if God did not have power over sin: He *Himself* reserves this sphere of freedom for man; He Himself, after all, in the creation of man in His own image made him a free counterpart of Himself — man who can defy Him, who can rebel against Him. The treachery of Judas is no doubt a means in the hand of the redemptive God; indeed, the treachery of Judas is even an element in His eternal plan of salvation; but at this point, where human logic would like to go farther and draw the conclusion — that consequently God Himself is the actual originator of evil, the real perpetrator — it stops and says ' no.' Never! Man alone is responsible for evil, man carries the full responsibility for sin; he received from God as part of his freedom the power to sin, but the misuse of this power is entirely his own act.

Just as little use is made in the New Testament of the idea of the power of sin and of the universal hold of sin on humanity, in the sense that thus in some way, as the judges say, the single individual is less accountable for his sin. The power of sin is indeed a superior force, one which dominates all mankind; but this superior power of sin is man's own fault. Nor can the idea of the Devil and of the evil powers of the unseen world be used to lessen man's responsibility. Nowhere is man represented as the innocent or all too unfortunate victim overpowered by an evil superior force through no fault of his own, as occurs in the Greek tragedies. Not sympathy, but the severity of judgment and redeeming compassion are the lot of sinful man.

That man is thus held fully accountable for sin is a decisive proof of the inviolable nature of the basic Biblical idea that man is actually and genuinely, not only apparently, God's free counterpart. Sin is indeed itself slavery, and to be sunk in sin is to be incapable of good. But this is the consequence of sin, not its cause. Even while each human being is seen in his immediate relation to God, he is also seen as one who is jointly responsible for the entire history of sin. If he is the slave of sin now, he himself is to blame for his condition.

The sinful state never becomes the explanatory and accordingly excusable cause of the sinful act; for the sinful state is itself act. Even the idea of slavery to sin cannot therefore be allowed to conceal that of freedom of decision and the concomitant responsibility. Freedom of decision and inability to decide now for the good are two sides of one and the same human reality, the one turned toward creation, the other toward eternal death. And both are presuppositions for the Biblical doctrine of redemption.

CHAPTER FIVE

*The Biblical Understanding
of Truth and Doctrine (Continued)*

CHAPTER FIVE

The Biblical Understanding
of Truth and Doctrine (Continued)

5. *Why Christ?* The Christian faith, most simply expressed, is *faith in Jesus Christ*. The Church would have done well if it had always withdrawn from involved doctrinal controversies to this simple confession of faith which alone is explicitly contained in the New Testament: Jesus Christ the Lord, Jesus Christ the Son of God, the Redeemer. For in this simple confession the nature of the Christian faith appears with complete clarity — it is trust in and obedience to the personally present Lord. Faith is not primarily faith in something true — not even in the truth ' that ' Jesus is the Son of God; but it is primarily trust in and obedience to this Lord and Redeemer Himself, and on the ground of this trust fellowship with Him according to His Word: ' Behold I am with you to the end of the world.' Fellowship with the living Lord who is present with us: this is what faith in Christ in the New Testament pre-eminently means.

It is precisely this formulation which gives rise to the question: Why Christ after all? Why not simply God? How can we understand faith in a mediator as the expression of personal correspondence? Here too we can confidently expect to get a twofold elucidation of our thesis as well as of the

New Testament testimony about Christ, because our thesis itself was obtained by using this testimony as starting point for our inquiry. To say that Jesus Christ is the content of faith, of truth, is a radical departure from the ordinary conception of truth. This is expressed in critical passages in the New Testament itself; in the prologue to the Gospel of John we read: 'But grace and truth came into being through Jesus Christ.' Truth came into being! For one schooled in the Greek conception of truth this phrase is utterly perverse. Truth, after all, is precisely that which is timeless, the changeless which is subject to the eternal. For truth to *come into being* is a contradiction in terms. But truth which has come into being is the very core of the Biblical message. Truth is something which *happens,* which God *does.* Truth and grace can be spoken with the same breath: truth like grace is encounter between God and man; grace and truth came into being in Jesus Christ.

The presupposition of this tenet follows in the prologue of the Fourth Gospel: 'No man has seen God at any time.' God, apart from his revelation in the form of a human being, is mystery. What we speculate about God is idolatrous interpretation of the divine mystery, of which we are all aware. The personal God can be known only in His personal revelation, and His personal revelation is the Incarnation of the Word. The Incarnation of the eternal Son of God is the unveiling of His quality of being Person and hence at the same time His will to fellowship. For this is the Biblical conception of God's quality of being Person: love, self-communication — that love which through all eternity the Father has for the Son, and the Son for the Father. God's quality of being Person, revealed in Jesus Christ, is itself of such a nature that it establishes fellowship. Being person [*Person-sein*] and being in fellowship [*In-Gemeinschaft-Sein*] are identical. Such is the Biblical concept of the Personality of God. The revelation of Himself as Person is therefore at the same time revelation of Himself as Love; consequently truth and grace are the same. Not only are truth and grace manifested in Jesus Christ, but in Him their real intentionality comes to realization. Jesus Christ not only reveals, He at once fulfills and realizes the Will of God. Hence ' we saw in Him the *Doxa Theou*, the *Gloria Dei*, the majesty of God.' The Incarnation of the Son is not only redemptive fact, but at the same time the realization of the divine world plan, the *oikonomia*, that is to say, the divine realization of the eternal purpose to comprehend the universe in Christ as its head. We may not divide the Nature from the Will of God, as if they somehow were separable. His Will is His Nature; and His Nature, His Will. Hence we may not talk about God without at the same time talking about His Will, and what is meant by His Will can be briefly stated: the Kingdom of God, revealed and grounded in the incarnate Son. The Incarnation is not only our Lord's taking the form of a servant because of sin: at the same time it is majesty, because it is the realization of the divine world plan. It is the concretion of God's will to have a counterpart in whom His Nature and His Love are reflected and answer Him. In Jesus Christ,

God reveals Himself as the God who approaches man, the God who because His Nature is Love wills that man answer Him in love — in that love which He Himself as Creator and Redeemer gives him. The event of the Incarnation marks the coming into existence of truth and grace.

The Work of the Redeemer. Nevertheless I believe that the ancient Christian development of dogma did not quite remain on the track of the Biblical revelation. The Incarnation as such is not the pivotal point of the Biblical revelation, but rather the *work* of the Redeemer. Jesus Christ did not come merely to come, but He came to redeem. To be sure, only the Incarnate Lord — very God, very man — can be the Redeemer. But the Bible guides us to ponder less the secret of the Person of Jesus than the mystery of His work. Let me reiterate once more that apparent commonplace: not the substantive, but the verb is the chief word in Biblical language. The old Christian theology converted the Biblical verb-theology into a Greek substantive-theology. That is the Platonic, substantialist element in it. The Bible is never substantialist, but always actualistic. It is essentially historical; but the contemplation of the Nature of Christ misleads to a certain Naturalism.

I must correct at this point certain emphases in my own book *The Mediator*. It was indubitably an unconditional necessity for the Church to defend the unity of God and man in Jesus Christ against all mythological, gnostic, and moralistic-rationalistic attacks. But the Church bogged (so to say) at that point. It gave the Christian faith a false orientation about the Being instead of the work of Christ. In this way it imperiled the fundamental historical character of the evangelical message by means of a static Platonism. The Person of the Mediator must also be understood as an *act* of God, namely, as His coming to us in revelation and redemption. It must be understood as the divine act of turning Himself toward and giving Himself to man. In this sense Melanchthon's famous word, ' To know His acts of kindness is to know Christ,' signifies a decisive return to the Biblical understanding of Christ. We should compare with this statement the main Christological passages in the Pauline Epistles, and we shall find it confirmed that predominant in the Biblical message is the movement, the coming down, the sending of the Son to us, His self-giving for us, His taking on Himself the form of a servant, His taking on Himself the sinful flesh, above all His suffering, dying, and rising again, His obeying, His loving and revealing, His expiating and redeeming. Even the Person of the Mediator is comprehended with the verb, if I may so express it, not with the substantive. One could actually say: Jesus Christ, even and especially in His divine-human *being* as Person, is God's *act*, just as He is the *Word* of God. In Him — not only through Him — does God *do* something to us. In Him, God reveals Himself; in Him, God reconciles the world unto Himself; in Him, God redeems us. Consequently in this connection too, where we are considering the Person, the mystery of the Person of Christ, what is essential is not something as it is in itself [*Ansichseiendes*], a divine-human Person as He is Himself [*Person-an-Sich*], but the relation of God, the dealing of God with the sinful and lost humanity, the revelatory and redemptive *act* of God.

The Name of Christ. Perhaps we can understand this whole point of view best if we begin by discussing the *name of Christ* itself. The Mediator has a functional name — the Messiah, through whom God rules and who carries into effect God's will to Lordship. Think of the parable of the Wicked Husbandmen, which I have already mentioned in another connection: the disobedient tenants who have usurped the seignioral rights are to be led back to obedience by the messengers of the Lord. Finally he sends his own son with the same intention. The son is no messenger: He is the will of the lord himself, personally present. In him the lord stretches out his hands toward the property which has been wrested from him. Jesus Christ as the Messiah is restorer of the Lordship of God, the Kingship of God. *The office,* his function, gives Him His name; God comes to us in His Son, in order to realize His Kingdom. Correspondingly, the first Christian creed apart from the Messianic name is the confession: He is the Lord. *Kyrios Christos.* In this Person the will to Lordship and the lordly power of God meet us. Jesus is the personified and incarnate kingly Will of God; God's kingly Will becomes a human person. To believe in Him thus means primarily that one bows to His Sovereign Will as God's Will in order to become obedient to Him.

This becomes especially clear in the Johannine concept: Jesus is *the Word of God.* What God says to us is this Person. In Him, God speaks to us His will, His intention, His decree, His world-plan, His love. Unlike the prophets, He is not the conveyer of a word, a message — the prophet after all is nothing himself; not He, but his message is important — He Himself is the message, His Person is God's revelatory doing. He Himself, *in persona*, is the self-communication of God; consequently we must always grasp the being and doing, the acts, words, and Passion of the Lord as a totality. He Himself therefore is the meeting with God (so to say); or, as the Old Testament believers expressed it, He Himself is God's visitation to men, God's coming near, God coming to us, Immanuel. In Him, God opens to us the mystery of Himself. 'Who sees me, sees the Father.' He is the Father made visible — obviously not to the corporeal eye, but to the eye of faith. God's words were already given through the prophets; but these words were detached from the Speaker Himself. The prophets, if asked about the Speaker Himself, had to point away from themselves to the distant God. Hence all prophecy is still unfulfilled revelation of God. What is lacking is unity between what is said and the presence of the Speaker. Precisely this thought is expressed in the sentence: He Himself is God's Word. When questions are now put about the One speaking, about the authority standing behind the Word, He no longer needs to point to the far-distant God, but may say: 'But I say unto you, Come unto me.' God's Lordship, previously only near to man, in Him is made directly accessible.

The Priestly Office of Christ. The third 'office' of Christ, according to traditional interpretation based on Scripture, is

the priestly office. Again the entire emphasis is upon the
doing and giving of God. To clarify the idea that Jesus
Christ is God's act of atonement, the Old Testament idea of
sacrifice is used. It is a two-sided happening, an active and
a passive — the priest sacrifices and the lamb is sacrificed.
The New Testament says of Jesus: He is both priest and lamb
at the same time, the One sacrificing and the One sacrificed.
For He sacrifices Himself. As in the Messianic title God's
will to Lordship is meant above all else, so here God's will to
fellowship. The concern is about ' the office creating the
atonement,' by means of which what has been estranged shall
be reconciled. That which divides is sin with respect to man,
the wrath of God with respect to God. But it is never said
that God is reconciled, but rather that God gives Himself in
His Son for the reconciliation of the world unto Himself.
Even in the suffering of Christ, God is the active and giving,
never the receiving part. God receives nothing which reconciles Him — not even a sacrifice agreeable to Him; such an
interpretation of the atonement cannot claim Biblical support. But God Himself gives Himself in the Son; the suffering of Christ is the act of God, namely, His giving, His giving
of Himself, by which He establishes fellowship.

We said at the start that in love, in the self-communication
of God to mankind, God's will to Lordship, His self-realization, comes to fulfillment. Similarly we can and must say
that the entire revelation and realization of the divine Will
reaches its culmination in this giving of Himself in Christ.
For in this way God establishes fellowship, and fellowship is
His real goal. In His self-giving to mankind in the Cross of

Christ, God reveals to us not only the most profound mystery of His heart — His love, His compassion — but He also creates that which is His cardinal concern, namely, fellowship, even while He gets rid of that which divides, namely, sin. The Person of the Mediator may never be understood apart from what He does in His suffering: ' Behold the Lamb of God, who taketh away the sins of the world.' The happening on the cross is the happening in which fellowship is established, the establishment of the ' new covenant in His blood.' Here the truth which God wills to reveal to us happens, a truth which He wills not only to reveal to us but also to *make actual* as fellowship and grace.

On this event in its concrete uniqueness, this Good Friday event (seen in the light of the subsequent Easter) — this ' accidental historical fact,' as Lessing called it — depends everything that we have said about the fundamental Biblical category: personal correspondence. Indeed, everything in the Bible is seen with reference to this basic category and bears testimony to it. But its essential meaning — the radical nature of this relation (the unconditioned *will* to Lordship and *will* to fellowship) and also the radical nature of the act establishing the relation — is fulfilled only in this unique event, and hence is understandable only with respect to it. We are dealing here with God's relation to mankind, a relation which is God's acting in space and time and therefore action in history. God's relation to the world and to mankind is not something timeless, but it is action in history. Its historicity is as unconditional as the relation itself: hence this event is unique; it happened ' once for all.' Its uniqueness is as essential to this Good Friday event as the unconditioned will to Lordship and fellowship of that love which is disclosed in this unique event.

The Two-sided Nature of Fellowship. But we should quite destroy the whole meaning of our thesis if we were to stop at this point. For our thesis states that correspondence is demanded, that the Will of God is fulfilled only when man's answer in response to God's Word has been given. For this reason the Bible never speaks of the objective event ' Christ ' by itself, but always at the same time of responding faith. ' For God so loved the world, that He gave His only begotten Son, *that whosoever believeth in Him shall not perish.*' ' But the righteousness of God is revealed without the help of the Law, namely *the righteousness through faith for all believers.*' It is not as if this response, this answer to the Word of God, were something secondary and additional — as someone has said, ' a thousand meters lower ' than that which God has done in Jesus Christ; but faith is spoken of on precisely the same level as Jesus Christ — so much so that Paul uses the two expressions ' righteousness of God ' and ' righteousness of faith ' interchangeably. If this faith is not reached, that also has not happened for which Jesus Christ came and suffered: the atonement, the fellowship between God and man. For this reason he whose responsibility it is to preach atonement in Christ must appeal with all possible urgency: ' Be *ye* reconciled! ' The effects of the current are in evidence only when the circuit is closed. Fellowship, then, is a two-sided happening; the ' yes ' of man is precisely as nec-

essary as the 'yes' of God. Without faith there is no atonement and no redemption. If one counts the passages in the
New Testament that speak of faith or in a similar sense of
repentance, conversion, love to God, turning toward God, and
what otherwise expresses the response of man, one recognizes
how the meaning and truth of everything depends upon both
sides and their correspondence. In fact one can say: *Faith is
the truth.* For what God wills is that His name be hallowed,
that His love find reciprocal love in man. To this end He
gave His Son, that this could happen, *that by means of His
self-giving, man would be led to self-surrender.*

6. *The Preaching of Repentance.* This refers firstly to the
surrender of the sinful will which is estranged from God and
in opposition to His Will. God does not will the death of the
sinner, we are told, but that he be converted. *Conversion* is
first of all turning away from and repulsion of what is inimical
to God, throwing away and negating the negative. Man must
stop on the way he is going and must turn around. Everything depends upon whether or not this happens.

The preaching of repentance is therefore the first task.
With it the Gospel of Jesus Christ begins, not only in the
preaching of repentance by John the Baptist but also by Jesus
Himself. 'Repent, for the Kingdom of Heaven is at hand.'
In repentance and conversion we find especially what we
called before the divine conditional: 'If ye are converted,'
'If the ungodly is converted,' 'If he turns himself toward the
Lord'; or, in another grammatical form: 'But he who is con-
verted,' 'But he who believes,' 'Who repents,' and so forth.

The unreadiness to repent inevitably brings upon itself the wrath of God. Indeed, the divine grace itself becomes judgment where it is not met with readiness to repent.

With the concept of repentance or conversion the same radical change occurred in the New Testament as with all other concepts, and in this Paul also is pioneer. As in the grace of God not only a word is given by Him but He Himself gives Himself in the Son, so the corresponding repentance can mean not only a change of disposition but man's surrender of himself. ' Ye are baptized into the death of Christ and hence also through His baptism into His death are buried with Him.' As on God's side a death is involved, so is it also on the side of man. The old man must die, he must be put off, he must be annihilated. And, indeed, man must of himself enter into this death. But while depicting this personal correspondence, Paul protects it from a serious misunderstanding. We have said that this correspondence is not equal on both sides. God is always first and the Giver; man always second, the one receiving. In the same way the death which *we* die is Christ's death; in *His* death we are baptized, in *His* dying we are included. He Himself draws us into His death. To die with Him is therefore the work of grace; it is not man's own work.

But this does not mean an occurrence in which man is merely involuntary and passive. Man must go to this death himself, and with his whole self. He himself must consent to what happens to him; indeed, it takes place only by means of his consent. God's gift is of such a nature that it must become actual in a voluntary act of man, in obedience and trust. Man cannot do this of himself, but only when gripped by the love of God and the holiness of God, expressed in Jesus' death. But he must *himself* agree with the act of being gripped and reconciled. To be gripped is at the same time to grip: repentance is at the same time an act of faith. It must therefore be an honest penitence, a genuine repentance. God wants a free and wholehearted ' yes,' and in this ' yes ' a ' no ' which surrenders the whole man to God, which separates the whole man from sin. ' So ye should consider yourselves as those who are dead to sin, but live for God in Christ Jesus.' The whole person must surrender himself; hence the expression ' death ' is the right word. Repentance means that I accept the death of Jesus Christ as a divine judgment upon myself and understand God's sentence of death, consummated in Him, as being vicarious, and therefore a sentence which really should fall on me — and yet at once exempts me. In the sixth chapter of Romans Paul develops the concept of repentance in its final, most radical form: the death of Christ corresponds to the death of man; the death of Christ must occur in order that this necessary death of man can also take place; the death of Christ is the actual stimulus in this happening to man, and yet at the same time it must happen as man's own decision; he himself must consent to this death.

7. *The Biblical Understanding of Faith.* While he is consenting to this death, he renounces what separated him from God, and he therefore participates in the life of God which in Jesus Christ the risen Lord is given to him as a Presence. This is *faith* in the essential, positive meaning of the word,

just as repentance is faith in a negative sense. Faith is resurrection with Christ to a new life. Faith, therefore, is not merely 'believing something,' but faith is a real happening which grips the whole person: coming into fellowship with the Redeemer, a genuine participation in His resurrection life. Faith means to be born again to a new life, to walk in the Spirit, to become implanted in Christ, to become a member of His body. Faith is, therefore, a genuine alteration of the person; indeed, a transformation of the person. Faith is the same as rebirth. The New Testament thus has made the concept of faith a radical one. As repentance is the death of the person who has deserted God, so faith is becoming a new person. In the Old Testament it is still called a new heart; but in the New Testament, a new man. Only that faith counts which is a new birth. We also see on the human side of the relation of correspondence how radically the conception of truth is changed. Even as the personal Word, the Son, took the place of abstract truth, so becoming a new person has taken the place of knowledge of truth.

And, indeed, this new being is one in fellowship or, therefore, a being in love, i.e., in the love of Christ. This, in turn, means participation in that mysterious being which goes from the everlasting Father to the everlasting Son through the Holy Spirit. What is of moment here is not union but fellowship. Subject and object may become one in a highest act of knowledge. The mystical experience of identification lies in the direction of knowledge, but it does not lie in the direction of faith. Faith should eventuate, not in union, but in fellowship. Fellowship is not, as abstract thinking always supposes, a form of union as yet unfulfilled. Fellowship is much more than — indeed, something quite different from — union. Union, in the last analysis, is being alone and living for oneself, but fellowship is being with another and living for him. The highest expression of fellowship in faith therefore means: to live for the Lord, to be instrument, to be servant — and yet at the same time to be child and son.

This Biblical understanding of faith, which is tantamount to what has been said about personal correspondence, stands in sharp contrast to the popular conception of faith. The latter is the product of the orthodox-Objectivistic confusion of Word of God and doctrine. From the middle of the second century the Church has instructed its believers that one ' must believe ' this and that doctrine in order to be a Christian — ' whoever wishes to be saved must, above all things, embrace the Catholic faith.' Once let dogma be the object of faith, and faith is then determined by means of the Object-Subject antithesis, by means of the rational concept of truth, and remains thus, even though the dogma is applied as revealed truth. Nor is this circumstance changed in the least if for dogma a passage from the Bible is used as ' revealed truth.' Fundamentally Bible-Orthodoxy is precisely the same as dogma-Orthodoxy, involving the application of the general concept of truth to revelation, instead of surmounting this understanding of truth by means of revelation. Where this confusion once dominates the understanding of truth, all subsequent instruction that faith is not only holding something as true but is 'also' trust and obedience is futile. It comes too late; the damage is already done: From being a fellowship of disciples the Church has become a school.

This misunderstanding of faith is noticeable in the fact that what in the Bible is meant as expression and description of the nature of faith has come to be understood as the object of faith. The Bible means that he who stands in faith is a new creature; the misunderstanding is that one must have faith in order to become a new creature through faith. The Scriptures say that he who stands in genuine faith *has* the Holy Spirit and experiences the Spirit's living, renewing action; the misunderstanding is that one must *believe that* through faith he receives the Holy Spirit and that the Spirit is an animating, renewing power. The apostles speak of the ecclesia as something to be experienced, manifested in its workings and achieving community and the fellowship of believers in the exchange of gifts; the misunderstanding considers the Church as the *object* of faith and even emphasizes that the *communio sanctorum* cannot be experienced. The Bible speaks about faith being the same as being in reality allied to Christ; the misunderstanding replaces the real alliance by the alliance with Christ as *object* of faith, as a truth to be believed. This confusion, this replacing of personal understanding of faith by the intellectual, is probably the most fatal occurrence within the entire history of the Church. It has been the cause of the too rapid expansion of Christianity and Ecclesiasticism, which has so heavily encumbered the testimony about the revelation of salvation in Jesus Christ, and has lessened respect for the Church more than anything else.

For this basic ecclesiastical evil is the hidden cause of all others. Even the Reformation was not so free from this confusion of God's Word and doctrine that it could have completely freed the Church from it, although the Reformers came close to overcoming it in their understanding of justifying faith.

8. *Justification and Sanctification.* But the Objectivistic displacement took place very early within this central period of the revival of faith, as we noted in the third chapter. The purely transcendent or forensic comprehension of *justification* is as much cause as effect of confusing the personal with the intellectual concept of faith. For Orthodox faith justification is something to believe, a truth pronounced by God Himself, a judicial sentence which at once absolves me and imparts to me the righteousness of Christ, a correct transaction before God's court of justice. What for Paul was a parable alongside other parables — i.e., the depiction of the divine transaction of judgment — in this context is taken literally by Orthodoxy and understood as being conceptually adequate. In this way that ' something,' which for Paul only pointed to the merciful God Himself who establishes fellowship with me, becomes the chief matter, the object of faith. Faith seizes this something offered by God, this being absolved and having imparted to one the righteousness of Christ, as a ' good ' proffered by God; it has to do with this truth, not with God Himself; this is faith in the dogma of justification as uttered by God Himself. That the doctrine of the mystical union and of sanctification *follows* immediately cannot repair the dam-

age already done. This elaboration into a scheme of salvation, into a series of different phases of a process, only indicates that one is trying to join together again what in the New Testament is a unity, after it has first been separated. The division of this unity into three phases — justification, unification, sanctification — is the attempt to counterfeit within the concept of truth determined by the Object-Subject antithesis what really lies outside its ken, namely, genuine personal encounter which establishes fellowship.

In the Pauline proclamation ' justification, unification and sanctification ' are one and the same seen from different sides, not a series of phases. In Christ, God Himself lays His hand on me, He opens Himself to me and opens myself to Himself, He breaks through to me through the wall of my selfish I-isolation. He establishes fellowship with me and thereby at once becomes my Lord. That Christ is my righteousness is the same as that Christ is my life; the righteousness of God is no other than the new obedience. That I turn from self to Christ is itself already the new life; that through faith I participate in the love of God which is in Christ is already the love of God poured out in my heart through the Holy Spirit. Nowhere in this context does faith depend on a ' something ' — not even on the ' something ' of justification — but only on Christ himself; for this reason Paul can pass from the ' juridical ' to the ' mystical ' formulation in the very same sentence: ' Through the law I am dead to the law, since I love God. I am crucified with Christ; I live, and yet no longer I, but Christ liveth in me.' Who would attempt in this context to separate justification, unification, and sanctification? Who would say which is first, which second, which third? Once one is gripped by faith, everything is contained in Christ — justification, unification, and the new life as life for Christ, instead of life for oneself.

When one stops dead with doctrine — even though it be divine doctrine — and does not advance to the reality signified ' in, with, and under ' the doctrine, it is only consistent that one distinctly places sanctification, the new life as life in love, ' over against ' justification as the ' essential object of faith,' as something which is not only second but also secondary.

In Orthodoxy, quite contrariwise to the New Testament, there is much more and much more forcible talk about faith than about love. It is after all Orthodoxy which gives the pattern for this whole understanding of the Gospel. If only your support of doctrine is clear and unequivocal, you are a Christian — however you may have disposed of the matter of love. That ' faith ' means to live for Christ as you trust Christ is forgotten; one now allows himself to relativize in a measure the attainment of the new life in Christ, that even the dead ' letter-faith ' is considered valid as faith. The last step in this direction was reserved for the most recent times: the doctrine of the invisibility of the fruits of the Spirit.

In the New Testament it is true that the root is hidden — the life with Christ in faith — but not what grows out of this root, the new life; the sap but not the fruit. For to believe ' in ' the new life has no value since faith is *itself* the new life. This new life is not something to be believed in but is itself experience of faith in Christ, who is present in the Word.

The fruits of faith or of the Spirit are therefore precisely the tokens of faith becoming visible. By comparison with them one can determine whether one really stands in living faith or whether faith is only a matter of the head, a purely intellectual matter, a faith in the dimension of ' believing something true.' Whenever one knows of no other except this faith there is nothing to say about the fruits of faith — for this intellectual faith yields no fruit. In this way the fruits of faith are changed from being a *demonstration* of faith to an *object* of faith, and therewith the opportunity is also lost to test the genuineness of faith. It is further consistent if this testing of the genuineness of faith, ever and again pointed out by the apostles as something contradictory to the essence of faith, is suspect. How could it be otherwise when one has made of a demonstration and sign of faith an object of faith? This intellectualistic transformation of the concept of faith brings to the Church the possibility of recognizing its poverty of faith by means of its lack of the fruits of faith.

9. *The Church as Correlate to the Word of God.* While we were speaking of faith and of the believer we elaborated an abstraction, which was necessary in the interest of clarity but which must now be resolved. This faith or this believer does not exist in itself or in himself. When the Bible speaks of the new life it speaks of life *in the community*, of life in the body whose head is Christ. Here too we shall have the task of settling misunderstandings which are determined through the false conception of truth, through the Object-Subject antithesis. We are dealing here with a misunderstanding of

the Church which is eighteen hundred years old. When the man in the street today hears about the Church — be he Catholic or Protestant or what not — he thinks of an institution, a Something which similarly to the State (even though in a different way) hovers over the individual, which has its own law and its own importance; a Something which men use for specific purposes or which they serve with a particular aim; a Something impersonal which, however, has significance for persons and their lives, and so forth. This concept of the Church as institution roots in an Objectivistic thinking which began already in the early days of the Church and finally led to the complete transformation of what in the New Testament is called *ecclesia*. To state this from the start in an entirely clear, unmistakable way: *The New Testament knows nothing of a Church as institution.* In the New Testament ' Church ' means only one thing: the people of God, the community of the holy, the elected, the gathering of believers, believers gathered together. Not even the slightest abstraction has any part in what the apostles called Church. Church is a concept understood purely and without exception as *personal*. Church is never anything else than the persons who through Christ, through fellowship with the living Lord, are themselves bound together into a living fellowship.

The Reformers again gave this New Testament idea of the Church to the world, in which for centuries it had been obscured by an entirely differently conditioned, sacral-institutional concept and, above all, through a strange ecclesiastical actuality. But their knowledge had the power to succeed only in a very partial degree; the old institutional concept of the Church, after Luther had penetrated through it and fought it with the greatest clarity and energy as error, forced its way back even into the Protestant Church, and the loophole through which it slipped back was the differentiating of visible and invisible Church. The New Testament community in a certain sense no doubt also differentiated between the visible and invisible Church — in the sense that even among the true members of the body there were also here and there false members, that is, those who belonged not genuinely but only apparently to the Body of Christ. But with the Church as institution this differentiation has not the least to do. One appeals for justification of the understanding of the Church as institution to the offices and the Sacraments just as to the Word of God given to the Church. This is entirely incorrect. To be sure, the community has offices and Sacraments and must have them necessarily; but they *are* not the Church, any more than I myself *am* an instrument which I have and use — even though it be an instrument of the utmost importance to life itself and given to me by God. The Church *has* offices, it *uses* Sacraments; it therefore *has* institutions — if one wishes to place offices and Sacraments into this category — but it *is* no institution. The Church also has its rules and needs them; but the Church *is* no set of rules, and the rules of the Church do not constitute the Church. In the New Testament the Church is never anything else than the community of those who belong to Christ through faith, whom through His Word and Spirit He has constituted the community.

The Church is therefore a magnitude to be understood as

completely personal; it is the genuine correlate to the Word of God, which Jesus Christ Himself is. The New Testament expresses this by means of the simile of body and members, of head and body: wherever Jesus Christ lives among men as Lord, as their Lord, there is the Church. Consequently the creation of the Church and nothing else is of moment in this age. It is more correct to say that what is of moment is the creation of the Church as the creation of faith or of believers, because the fellowship-establishing Word and work of Jesus corresponds to the actual fellowship and not to the individual person or his faith. Jesus wills to hold man, the person — and he holds him through His Word in faith. But Jesus wills to hold man in fellowship, and again He holds him through His Word and the Spirit. Faith is nothing other than to become a member in the body of Christ. While the individual is released from his I-isolation, out of the sin which estranges him from God and man, he is taken into fellowship with God and at the same time with man. And, contrariwise, he will not be released in any other way from his I-isolation, except as he is taken into the concrete fellowship. The Word of God does not move aimlessly; even as the Word became flesh in Jesus of Nazareth, so it wills to work further as historical Word carried in man, as the faith-awakening witness-word of those who pass on to others what they have received. It is only by means of such a witness-word from other men that faith can come into being in any man. Through the Incarnation of the Word, God Himself bound Himself to the historical Word, in order therewith also to bind us to this historical Word and in Him to our fellows. As God Himself enters history in His Son, so man is to be incorporated into the historical fellowship of believers.

The relation between the Word of God and the Church is thus again that of personal correspondence. Paul once pointed this out with the simile of marriage. As the man gives himself to the woman and the woman to the man in human-natural love, so Christ gives Himself to the community and the community to Christ in divine love. But again this correspondence does not signify identity. The relation of Christ to the community is quite different from the converse. Christ here too is inexchangeably the first, the One giving, creating, originating; the community is the established, the receiving, the created part. Christ is the Lord, the Head, from whom comes all life and all guidance; the community is the body, which receives its life and direction from the Head. And yet it is not simply the product of the Head, as in the cause-effect scheme something is the product of something else. Between the community and Christ obtains a relation *sui generis*; namely, that of trusting obedience and of responding love, even as this same relation obtains among the members, that one serve the other in love. It is thus in the Church that the consummate goal of God shines forth: the *Kingdom of God*, in which God's love is all in all.

10. *The New Life.* And yet it only shines forth and is not yet present. The new life, the life from God, is not only promised, and to be believed in because it is promised. *This* eschatological interpretation of faith is again connected with the false Objectivistic concept of faith and its falsely under-

stood doctrine of justification. The New Testament makes clear that the new life is already present, just as certainly as that Jesus, the living Lord, dwells in us and that the Holy Spirit is given us as a pledge. It never says that we believe only in the promise of something which is future, rather, it declares that *in* faith we already *have* a real participation in what is future, in what is coming. But the consummation of what is coming is yet unrealized. For this reason faith of necessity becomes *hope*. The Church and faith are designed to further God's eternal goal of salvation and consummation; for this goal of salvation and consummation is the content of the divine revelation.

In Christ, in the community the new life is a divinely achieved reality, is indeed the action of God, Himself present. But it is not yet what is solely real and what is solely efficacious. The body is still ' the body of sin,' not only in the physical but also in the social sense of the word. We yet live as a fellowship of believers in a sinful and perverse world. Sin is yet active within ourselves, and though conquered by means of the Spirit which dwells in us, is ever again sallying forth from its skulking place, from the ' body of sin,' into our life. Faith is assuredly the new life, but it is the new life struggling with the old. Consequently faith is not itself ultimate. Faith itself is waiting as hope for another, the real ultimate, the vision, when we shall see God face to face and shall know even as we are known, when we shall be like Him.

The Pledge of the Spirit.   The Bible never describes eternal life, but tells us plainly what its essential nature is. It is the *Gloria Dei,* and that means the perfect reflection of the divine holiness and the divine love in the creature — a creature who in order to be able to respond so fully to God's will must be newly created. For sinful corruption has penetrated to the very marrow of existence, but the earthly incompleteness as such is also a hindrance to attaining the final consummation. It is well expressed, ' Who believes in me, he has eternal life'; he ' will live, even though he die.' But eternal life cannot develop in a mortal body, the holy Will cannot fulfill itself in an actual person who is partly given to sin. The new life which we receive in faith is, after all, the life of the risen Christ: therefore, what has already been received, the Holy Spirit dwelling within us, is only the ' first stroke '; it is only the ' pledge ' of the resurrection life which fulfills itself. ' If the Spirit of Him who awakened Jesus from the dead lives in you, so He who awakened Christ from the dead will also make your mortal bodies immortal by means of His Spirit who lives in you.' The new is present but only in germ, upon the development of which through a new act of God we can only wait. But we can wait in certainty. For it is one and the same Spirit which dwells in us and which will awaken us.

Consummation. The goal from the point of view of the individual is ' to be like Him '; from the point of view of the community it is the Kingdom of God. The simile which the Bible uses for the latter is the meal — the convivial meal, the feast, or the wedding banquet — or the ' face-to-face vision.' In both ways of expression the same is meant: direct intercourse with God and through Him with one another. By means of this direct intercourse, however, we become as the Fourth Evangelist says, ' like Him.' The image of God, after which we are created, will then be consummated in us. God will thus effect His perfect Lordship and His perfect self-communication, and at the same time man will be perfected in that for which he is created and determined. The relation of personal correspondence is then fulfilled; truth is then realized as the perfect Presence of God with His creation and the perfect presence of the created with the Creator through Him who is the eternal Word and who through all eternity is stipulated for incarnation. For ' if Christ, our life, will be revealed, then ye too will be revealed with Him in glory.' If then not union but fellowship, which is rooted in God's self-communication, is truth, then this is the last word to be said, as it has been said.

CHAPTER SIX

The Biblical Understanding
of Truth and the Church

CHAPTER SIX

The Biblical Understanding of Truth and the Church

To some extent we are now in a position to understand according to its origin and to weigh according to its meaning the antithesis of Objectivism and Subjectivism from which we started in the first chapter. Objectivism is determined by the correct observation that in the creation of His connection with man God's act is first. The Creator is prior to and independent of His creation. The Word of God is prior to and independent of faith, God's act of atonement is prior to justifying faith, the call of the Church and its Sacraments is prior to the faith of the individual, the Bible is prior to the inspiration of the Holy Spirit. As the eternal Son takes human nature upon Himself in Jesus of Nazareth, not the contrary, so God's free action is always first and creative, man's answer is second and what is created.

All this Objectivism would maintain and place on a firm footing. Consequently what may be called the substance of the Church is always to some extent preserved with it, however great the damage may be which it causes. At any rate in Catholic Sacramentalism the Sacrament was perpetuated, in its Clericalism the Church, in its Dogmatism the Word of revelation — in some way these were always perpetuated, even if in a markedly distorted form, as in the Legalism of Pharisaism something of the holy Will of God was always safeguarded. Subjectivism is doubtless the genuine Church-dissolving tendency which more seriously jeopardized the welfare of the revelation, even though as reaction it has often had a certain beneficial effect and even though it was often in the form under which Biblical truth would blossom out against torpidity. Its relative power, if one would briefly express it, is the observation of the fact that God's free rule of the Spirit can be received by man only in an equally free spiritual act. Subjectivism, therefore, holds to the second basic fact of the relation of personal correspondence. It has no genuine substance because or in so far as it has isolated the basic fact, but it lives, so to say, by virtue of its opponent, Objectivism, as a protest movement. But to designate it as Protestantism for this reason, as happens time and time again, and therewith to understand the Reformation as an apparent form of this Subjectivism is (as we now know) to miss the point completely. Not every protest movement is Protestantism — and we should notice in addition that the very name Protestantism for the Reformation has an apocryphal origin and questionable value. As Objectivism leads to torpidity, so Subjectivism to dissolution. What is torpid can be awakened again to life; but what is dissolved is no longer in existence.

The Need of Coming to Terms with Objectivism. If in spite of what we have just said we wish critically to analyze only Objectivism in this lecture, we do so because the struggle against Legalism is the real struggle of the Church. Objectivism has always been the real ecclesiastical danger within the Church — through all centuries and even now. From within the Church its danger is much more difficult to recognize, and the struggle against it was always the most dangerous. For the opponent will feel himself attacked in his most sacred precinct and will consider himself called to be guardian on the battlefield of the holy treasure entrusted by God to the Church. Within the Church the struggle against false Ecclesiasticism and false faith in all times has been most necessary and most difficult. But we may not forget for a moment that even as we are now contending against one side, we also have the opponent on the other side in every era.

But we will not concern ourselves with ecclesiastical Objectivism in general, but with those of its appearances with which we ourselves have to deal in our own situation, namely, within the Churches of the Reformation and their theology. I should like to consider especially three such forms: Objectivism in doctrine; Objectivism in office; Objectivism in the Sacrament.

The Doctrine of the Divine Infallibility of Scriptural Texts. We have already dealt with *Objectivism in doctrine*, that is, with Orthodoxy, in detail and in review. We have yet to recognize several of the apparent results. Objectivism in doctrine consists in equating or failing to distinguish between God's Word and doctrine. This false identification is connected with the foundation of the Reformation Church, above all, with its relation to the Holy Scriptures. The mistake is not that Orthodoxy called the Bible, the entire Holy

Scriptures, the Word of God, but rather that in its tendency toward security it legalistically misunderstood this Bible-as-God's-Word in the sense of something disposable. The doctrine of the divine infallibility of Scriptural texts is a clear parallel to the doctrine of the infallibility of the Pope. The difficulties and corruption that developed therefrom in the Church are known. With this doctrine the Church got unto the path of a theological Docetism. As with the ancient Docetists the human nature of Christ was appearance, so in this connection the human nature through which the Word of God enters into the Bible was considered appearance. The word of Luther, that the Bible is the crib in which Christ lies, was not understood in all its profundity. Genuine Bible faith — because the Scripture is the cradle — self-evidently belongs together with Biblical criticism; for a Bible free from error would no longer be human, and, contrariwise, the recognition of the humanity of the Scriptures makes it more possible to distinguish the law, capable of error, from its divine infallible content. Through Orthodoxy, however, Biblical criticism as such is excluded and its application is abhorred as a sign of unbelief. The history of the disintegration of this orthodox view of doctrine is not without a certain tragic aspect. How much genuine Bible faith was spoiled or hindered or compromised through a false theory of the Bible! The Word of God could surely call out to the Church, ' For your sake my name is calumniated among all peoples.' For the fact that so many modern folk wish to have nothing more to do with the Bible, this false seeking for security must carry not a little of the blame. But this is all well known.

The History of Salvation Becomes the Doctrine of Salvation. Another misunderstanding connected with the first is less well known. By means of the identification of Word of God and doctrine, a specific ecclesiastical doctrinal system quite apart from verbal inspiration — mayhap the Lutheran or the Reformed doctrine — was equated with the Word of God in the Holy Scriptures. One simply disregarded the fact that the Bible gives us the Word of God in a multiplicity of doctrines in part very different and even contradictory. The Pauline theology is not the same as the Johannine or the Synoptic, the New Testament theology is not the same as the Old, and the priestly theology in the Old Testament is not the same as the prophetic. Whoever gives the Bible a chance to disclose its genuine meaning knows this, but classical Orthodoxy dare not admit it. It must therefore either ignore these differences in doctrine or explain them away through the use of allegorical interpretation. Genuine Bible faith intends to hear from the Scriptures the single, never contradictory Word of God, but it is free enough to recognize that this one Word manifests itself in very various doctrines: it does not identify Word of God and doctrine. But Orthodoxy does not recognize this distinction; paradoxically, it therefore actually falsifies the Scriptures which it intended to protect. That God can speak to us His single, never contradictory Word through the priestly writings of the Old Testament as well as through the prophetic or the New Testament writings, even though these several writings are very various and in part contradictory, just as He can speak His single, never contradictory Word through the contradictory accounts of Luke and Matthew in regard to this or that incident in the life of Jesus — this correct proposition was converted into the following false one: There are no contradictions in the Bible, either in statements or in doctrine; all such contradictions are only apparent, and can be resolved by means of the harmonizing or allegorizing interpretation. The hidden Docetism also becomes manifest in this connection. One does not believe in the genuine historicity of the divine revelation. One does not take seriously that actually in the Old Testament the fullness of knowledge was not yet present, the knowledge granted to us in the Word becoming flesh in Jesus Christ. The historical revelation is converted into a timeless system of truth. Wherever allegorizing is done, either the Platonic concept of truth or the Judaic Legalism is always at stake. The *history* of salvation is converted into a timeless *doctrine* of salvation.

What Is Meant by 'Proclamation'? A further consequence which necessarily follows from the basic error of Orthodoxy is the overvaluation of doctrine in the life of the Church and in the faith of the individual. The Church has received a holy vocation to teach because of the indissoluble sacramental connection between doctrine and Word of God. But the primary commission of the Church is not doctrine but proclamation. Proclamation, I suppose, must always have a doctrinal content, but it is itself something other than doctrine. It is faith-awakening, faith-furthering, faith-wooing address. Genuine proclamation always has a prophetic character — even if we preachers are no prophets; pure doctrine, on the other hand, has a didactic character. There is a kind of ' proclamation ' which is much more suitable for the Jewish synagogue than for the Christian Church, even though its doctrinal content is New Testament. The confusion of doctrine and Word of God gives to theology and to theological doctrinal disputes an altogether disproportionate importance. Not enough stress can be placed in the congregation upon doctrine and knowledge of doctrine; but the measure of doctrinal development which the individual and congregation can endure without suffering injury to their faith is always proportionate to the measure of practical realization of that faith. A congregation in which much living prayer and much hearty brotherly love is present can digest much doctrine; doctrine will nurture it in faith, in love, and in hope. But when faith has little strength practically to shape life, an overdose of doctrine is to that degree deadly. In this connection the Church, with its orthodox attitude, perpetrated egregious pedagogical errors, from the consequences of which it yet suffers. But whenever the proclamation itself is confused with doctrine, the Pauline assertion — ' faith comes out of proclamation ' — becomes poisonous. The Church then believes that it need only pile doctrine upon doctrine, without troubling about practical results and without noticing that in this way it kills souls instead of awakening them to a true life. It is high time that the Church again thought through its practice of preaching and instruction in the light of the knowledge that the traditional identification of doctrine and proclamation is a destructive error. The mistakes which follow from this basic error of Orthodoxy are not corrected by constantly alleging that the Word alone is efficacious. Of course the Word alone is efficacious, but doctrine is not — not even Biblical or catechetical doctrine. When we consider the Biblical understanding of proclamation, we observe that it means an event entirely personal, in the nature of a personal meeting, which is far different from the catechetical homiletical traffic in dogma which is determined by the Greek concept of truth.

What we ordinarily understand and employ as sermon and instruction is foreign to the Bible itself. The *missionary* proclamation of the apostles has only a distant relationship to what takes place in our preaching; and whether there was in the already existing congregation something analogous to our sermon is at least highly questionable in view of the portrayal in I Cor., ch. 14. This is not said to discredit the sermon as in the course of Church history it has become the form of proclamation, but rather to point out that this teaching nature of proclamation is linked with certain historical presuppositions; that, therefore, this kind of proclamation is not 'the' proclamation, but rather is one of many possible methods of proclamation, the particular serviceableness of which must be proved anew by the Church in every generation. The same obtains for 'instruction.' Numerous critical voices from within the Church itself are stressing the need for reflection about whether our traditional regulations for instruction are really ordained by God. The notion that instruction, hence the mediation of doctrine, is the best means to lead young people to faith is in any event difficult to verify in the Bible, and it does not seem that churchly practice has in any way furnished proof that it is. The general complaint about the pedagogical nuisance of our customary instruction is too widespread for one to fail to hear it.

Once let the relation between Word of God and doctrine be rightly understood, and there will hardly be room any longer for the view that the single thing which the Church could do for the awakening of faith is the conceptual clarification of the Holy Scriptures. Has it, then, not yet been noticed that the most perfect knowledge of Biblical concepts and the entire acceptance of Biblical doctrine is wholly compatible with the completest want of actual faith — and indeed that this is anything but a rare phenomenon? Need one always fail to notice that ' to speak the Word of God more distinctly' has very little to do with a yet more thorough theological indoctrination? The notion that the completest catechetical instruction, be it for adults or youth, is the best *way* to faith is the product of an undue stress upon logic — even though supernatural — which has very little to do with what the Bible itself calls ' proclaiming the Word of God.' It is much rather a consequence of that confusion between the two concepts of truth of which we have been speaking. The practice of the ancient Church as well as that of modern foreign missions and of evangelization seems to us to point another way: that the actual function of doctrine — the doctrinal sermon as well as instruction — normally belongs where there is already a confessional congregation, where the concern is no longer with establishing a believing congregation, but rather with strengthening faith and deepening knowledge of faith. But the proclamation which seeks to initiate faith is a form of the Word in human speech which is vastly different from the doctrinal presentation. This truth the Church must learn again from those who have worked in the sphere of missions and classic evangelization; but the Church will first be able to learn it when it has discerned as error the false identification of doctrine and Word of God. This is one consequence of our theological reflection, perhaps the weightiest and most practical.

The Sacrament of Baptism. The second question, *Objectivism in the understanding of the Sacraments,* leads us directly into actual and critical ecclesiastical problems. I must confine myself here to the sacrament of baptism. The old controversial question of whether the New Testament says anything about child baptism will not be raised now. Whether or no it does, the fact still remains that in those passages where baptism is spoken of didactically, where its significance is shown for faith and the Church, it takes place in this way, that the fact of baptism is a two-sided happening which conforms completely to what we have called personal correspondence. In baptism it is God, first and sovereign, who acts, who forgives sin, who cleanses man and regenerates him. But man too acts in baptism. He allows this cleansing of himself to take place, he lets himself be drawn into the death of Christ, he confesses his faith and his attachment to Christ. Baptism is not merely a gift to man, but also an active receiving and confession on the part of man. Indeed baptism, precisely as this free confession of man, is the stipulation for the individual's joining the Church. Baptism is not only an act of grace, but just as much an act of confession stemming from the act of grace.

In the Catholic doctrine and practice this sacrament became entirely separated from its original Biblical meaning. Baptism is an *opus operatum,* man is *object* of the divine act, grace in a sense is applied to him in a way which takes no account of the fact that the one being baptized is a subject; in certain exigencies unborn children are also baptized in the womb. Child baptism — more precisely infant baptism — really becomes normal and what is taken for granted.

The Reformation retained infant baptism on the basis of closely related ecclesiastical grounds. It found therein a particularly powerful testimony indicative of the anticipatory grace of God, on free election grounded purely in the goodness of God and not in man's disposition or circumstances. But in that way it encountered dogmatic and practical difficulties which heavily encumber Reformation Churches to this day. The principal proposition of the Reformation in the doctrine of the sacrament, which brought to sharp expression the opposite of the Catholic *opus operatum,* was *nullum sacramentum sine fide,* the inseparable intimate connection between sacrament and faith. To be sure, faith does not produce the sacrament; but the sacrament is not accomplished, it is no true sacrament, without the faith. Luther and his successors drew from this basic proposition the necessary conclusions for infant baptism. Grant that infant baptism is a genuine sacrament, that there is no uncertainty about it, and we admit that infants too have faith. Orthodox Lutherans assure us that the faith of the infant, in so far as it is genuine faith, lacks neither the knowledge of the Word nor assent or trust. Even Calvin defended this interpretation, though somewhat faintheartedly; but he certainly moved another idea into the foreground in accordance with the precedent of Zwingli: the idea of the Covenant. It is not so much the individual faith of the infant as, above all, the faith of the 'household' by means of which the baptized infant is qualified to be accepted into the Covenant of God. But both the Lutheran and Reformed trends of thought have their difficulties. In the first place, the concept of faith becomes unclear — for what does faith mean if we attribute knowledge, assent, and trust to an infant who otherwise is incapable of understanding or consent? But in the second place Covenant and body of Christ are separated. For even if by virtue of being a member of a Christian household one can in some way be reckoned as being in the Covenant of God, yet he can certainly not be considered as belonging to the body of Christ, to which none belongs except believers. Altogether devious is a new interpretation of the sacrament of baptism, in which in any event no question is asked about faith, whereby the speaking of the words of promise suffice for the sacrament as such. With this interpretation — in contrast to the classical Lutheran and Reformed one — personal correspondence is given up and the sacrament is equated with the missionary sermon.

Neither the Lutheran nor the Reformed Church found its settlement of the question of baptism entirely satisfactory. It was noticed that the New Testament declaration of baptism could be linked neither with the idea of infant faith nor

with that of Covenant faith by proxy of the parents and witnesses in their firm conviction [*Plērophoria*]. Something in
the relation of personal correspondence was disturbed, and
this feeling led to the introduction of confirmation, which
could not be Biblically grounded. In confirmation the missing factor of response in the New Testament baptism act was
recovered (so to say): the personal ' yes ' as man's answer
to God's promise of grace. The whole of the New Testament
act of baptism was thus divided into two parts: the objective
gift of grace in infant baptism and the subjective confession
of faith in confirmation. Although by and by confirmation
was introduced practically everywhere, this settlement too
never particularly pleased the Church. The statements of
the New Testament about baptism continued to be connected with infant baptism and yet the bad conscience roused
by this identification was soothed by completing baptism with
confirmation, which certainly does not stem from the Bible.

This difficulty increased, the more frequent and crass the
instances were where persons who had been baptized as infants and therefore were included in the Covenant of God
arrived at the power of making their own decisions and turned
their backs on the Church and the Christian faith. Most of
the contemporary neopagans and also most members of athe-
istic societies have been baptized as infants; what does the
grace of baptism, of which in any event they probably never
even heard, mean for them? What does the fact of having
been baptized mean for the large number of contemporary
people who do not know and do not even care to know
whether they have been baptized? Infant baptism, which has

its good points in an entirely Christian fellowship — that is to say, a fellowship of persons who all joyfully profess Jesus Christ as their Lord — becomes a highly questionable arrangement where it is requested more from consideration of custom than from conviction of faith. It becomes a questionable arrangement when judged on the basis of the undervalued fundamental assertion of the Reformation: *Nullum sacramentum sine fide* — the sacrament is not valid without faith. In this Reformation principle the basic Biblical fact of personal correspondence is again expressed.

In the contemporary Objectivist bent of theology the tendency is so prevalent to stress one-sidedly the objective element in baptism that there is no longer even any awareness of the difficulty of which we have been speaking. What is of concern is not faith, it is said, but only the divine word of promise which is spoken over the infant. Where one separates the Word of God and faith to this extent, the character of the *sacrament* is invalidated; then ineluctably the proposition of the Reformation holds: *Nullum sacramentum sine fide*. The word of promise spoken over the infant is then nothing other than a *sermon-word*; none inquires about the efficacy of the Word. But the sacrament of the New Testament is not only a sermon-word, but a bifrontal happening in which God says ' yes ' to man and man says ' yes ' to God.

None knows better than the missionary that this is true. I do not know of any evangelical mission where infants are baptized without decision; much rather with infants as with adults who are to be baptized the presuppositions of faith are inquired about, with the latter the individual himself being asked, with the former the 'household.' No children of unbelievers are baptized, only children of Christians; that is to say, one acts on the basis of the proposition: *Nullum sacramentum sine fide.* This was also the presupposition of the Reformation practice of baptism. All our ancient baptismal liturgies implicated as the essential element the confession of faith of the parents or the witnesses to the baptism, and the vow to provide Christian instruction for the one being baptized. This means that infant baptism will be undertaken only when, according to human measurements on the basis of the confession of faith, the proxy-faith of the persons responsible, the 'household,' can be examined beforehand. The furtherance of confession of faith and of responsibility for Christian instruction at that time led to no important conflicts, because, disregarding exceptions, everyone was ready to acknowledge the creed of the Church and instruction was obligatory. With the cessation of these historical conditions the presupposition also dropped away under which alone child baptism could be justified on the basis of the Bible — although this too, as we saw, was not without certain difficulties. The contemporary practice of infant baptism can hardly be regarded as being anything short of scandalous.

Visible and Invisible Church. This question of baptism of children is not a single question in the large complex of Church problems, but rather is decisive for the entire churchly practice since baptism is the basis for Church membership. He who has been baptized in the Lutheran or Reformed congregation belongs to the Lutheran or Reformed Church. The host of correctly baptized persons who within and without the Church have been completely alienated from it must therefore be reckoned as belonging to the Church. The Church, after all, in the course of the centuries, has utilized the objective factor so one-sidedly as criterion of itself — correct doctrine and right administration of the sacrament — that for long it has lacked the means or will to remove from its membership baptized persons who at heart are completely alienated from it. Objectivism in the concepts of sacrament and Church led to an expansion altogether too rapid which immediately must become manifest in directly tragic measures as soon as one is obliged to use personal criteria for Church membership; that is to say, therefore, as soon as anything like a personal confession is encouraged. Then the comparatively little group of believers separates itself from the mass of millions of baptized unbelievers or those disinterested in the Church. The Church up to this time a fiction becomes a fact.

By appealing to the difference between visible and invisible Church one may not legitimize theologically (so to speak) the people's Church of Constantine, to which everyone belonged and which had over against it no nonchurchly world. This justification of existing conditions, stemming from Augustine, overlooks two factors: first, that this differentiation between visible and invisible Church is also necessary in the purest confessional Church; and, secondly, that it may not be placed in opposition to the furtherance of the confessional Church. He who does not want to confess Christ does not belong in the Church. The Church can hardly separate with certainty genuine from spurious faith — God alone can do that, and therefore the true Church is invisible — but it can and should determine who intends to confess Christ and who not. The relinquishment of this encouragement for confession — indeed, the surrender of this confessional criterion — and the sufferance of manifest atheists in the Church is a relinquishment of an essential mark of the Church. Church discipline may never be concealed with an appeal to the necessary distinction between visible and invisible Church, which is of quite another dimension. The surrender of this essential characteristic is attended with a prodigiously serious displacement: the displacement of the concept of the Church from the personal to the institutional. Count among Church members such as openly do not confess Christ, and the Church can no longer be considered a community of believers, but only as an institution, an instrument for the development of the believing community. Perhaps this displacement was a practical necessity, perhaps this ' people's Church ' is still today something worth retaining, but then it must be made clear, and clearly taught, that by Church is understood something totally different from the Church of the New Testament and that this difference has nothing to do with the differentiation between visible and invisible Church. The ' Church ' as institution is not the ' visible ' one, and the Church in the personal sense is not the ' invisible ' one.

The Communio Sanctorum. We should also never forget that this too rapid expansion of the Church in large measure began with Constantine. For that is but to say that it stands in a reciprocal relation to the Objectivistic concepts of sacrament and Church of the early Catholic Church. One-sided Objectivism at all odds is a distinctive characteristic of the Catholic Church. The Church is understood not so much as *Communio sanctorum* as holy institution, sacramental establishment of grace, and hierarchical legal organization. Not the Word, but the sacrament and the office, is decisive, and the sacrament as *opus operatum* of the rightly ordained bearer of the priestly office is independent of faith. In the Reformation the contradistinction between this sacramental-ecclesiastical Objectivism and the New Testament testimony about faith and Church was recognized and asserted. Luther never wearied of reiterating in his era that the Church is nothing other than the *Communio sanctorum,* the group of believing Christians. The confessional congregation undoubtedly stemmed from the logical conclusion of the Lutheran concept of the Church — a conclusion which Calvin in his way drew through advancing public confession by the individual. But reasons arising from concern for the people's welfare argued for the preservation of the people's Church inherited from the time of Constantine. It was perpetuated by means of infant baptism, which really meant infant baptism commanded by public authorities and protected by penal sanctions: Woe to him to whom it should occur not to bring forward within the shortest possible time his newborn child for baptism! The compulsion fell away, but the custom remained after faith and the inner connection with the Church of Christ had long since disappeared. The discrepancy between these two Churches, the gigantic Church of those baptized and the tiny Church of those assenting to confession, is one of the chief causes of the present difficulties of the Church in all places. Seen in the long Church-historical perspective, the essence of the situation in which the present-day Church finds itself is above all the replacing of the people's Church of Constantine by the pre-Constantine Church of those making confession. If the Church again is a community of those who confess Christ, personal correspondence, despoiled by Objectivism, is again restored. The meaning of the Church as living in fellowship, confessing the Lord, can again become distinct. The fatal inheritance from Constantine is liquidated, and with it the false Objectivism in the understanding of the Church.

The right content in the idea of the people's Church, grounded in consideration for the developmental nature of faith, should in this way not be denied. The advance of the confessional Church easily leads to an individualism which is just as foreign to the New Testament Church as the institutional idea of the Church. Even if an infant and some adults, who indeed grew up in a Christian home but who have not really been gripped by the Word of God, cannot in the genuine sense be counted in the community of Christ, yet in a sense they belong in some way within the province of the Church so long as they do not directly in a negative decision dissociate themselves from it. This is what was really meant in the Reformed doctrine of baptism, with its reference to the Old Testament idea of the Covenant, and this is what was retained as its token in child baptism in spite of all its dogmatic difficulties. This trend of thought certainly does not destroy the personalistic idea of the Church, but, on the contrary, builds it up, yet gives it (with regard to the developmental nature of faith) a less rigorous interpretation in which this tendency reckons with a confession yet latent (so to speak), a preliminary form of genuine decisive faith. Account must be taken of the fact that the use which can be made of this less rigorous thought of the Covenant must be restricted by the degree to which the Church finds itself in the missionary situation, and to the extent that it does not live in the midst of a people who profess the Christian faith, but rather finds itself a minority among a people who are indifferent or hostile to the Church.

The third question can hardly be separated from the one just discussed, namely, Objectivism in the understanding of the office. The Protestant ecclesiastical office is much more strongly encumbered than is ordinarily granted with an ancient Catholic tradition of office which deviates from the New Testament. The circumstances are known through which in the second and third centuries the priest-bishop office developed. The New Testament recognizes no difference between clergy and laity, between a ' spiritual ' profession and a nonspiritual people of the Church. All are spiritual who are joined with Christ in faith through the Holy Spirit. As such they are also all active, not only in daily living but in the worship service of the congregation. Setting over against each other active-expending and passive-receiving parts of the Church is, as the fourteenth chapter of I Corinthians shows, unknown to the New Testament community. This un-

Biblical procedure is the correlate to the ancient Catholic, un-Biblical concepts of bishop and priest.

The New Testament Understanding of the Office and the Reformation. The New Testament, to be sure, knows ' offices ' in abundant differentiation and gradation: apostles, prophets, evangelists, teachers, the episcopate, the diaconate, elders. But entirely disregarding this fact, that the multiplicity and kind of these offices do not remotely correspond with those of the Reformation Church, they are also separated on the same basis from those of the later Church, in that they are wholly spiritual and nowhere determined by ecclesiastical law. The offices stand in a specific correlation to *charismata* and for that reason the efficacy of the office-bearer was definitely linked with his *charisma*, his divine endowment. Only at the end of the New Testament epoch, in a period about which we know through the post-Pauline pastoral epistles, the beginning of a canonical interpretation can be faintly traced. Not only in this regard, but in regard to various other criteria, it can be noticed that we stand at the border of ancient Catholicism. In this period bordering the New Testament epoch it is not yet possible to discover that a bearer of an office simply on the strength of its once having been conferred on him should have a specific authority, irrespective of his spiritual qualification and testing, solely by virtue of the canonical act of ordination. This concept of office is incompatible with the spirit of the New Testament.

In this respect the Reformation, going back to origins, substantially corrected the Catholic development in the wrong direction. But it did not carry this development to its logical conclusion; on the contrary, it very soon turned back to the Catholic trend because of practical considerations and because of the transformation in the understanding of the Church which set in early. The Reformation, to be sure, proclaimed the universal priesthood of all believers and fundamentally denied the difference between layman and religious; but it did not allow itself to draw the practical conclusion to this fundamental proposition: it hardly aspired toward reinstituting the general, active participation of members of the congregation in worship and the responsibility of all members for the functions of the body, not to speak of being able to put it into effect. The picture of the worshiping congregation in the Protestant Church, just as in the Catholic, is not as in Corinth the circle where each in succession made his contribution to the common edification, but actually what we understand by a Church service of worship, that one who gives stands up before the crowd of those who receive. The Protestant Church became a ' clergyman-church ' [*Pfarrerkirche*], a congregation in which in substance one man is responsible for all that the congregation does, and the rest therefore remain more or less without active responsibility. The Reformed Church no doubt connected in a significant way this one-sidedness of the ' clergyman-church ' with the presbytery and diaconate, but it too failed to lead back to origins.

Mistaken Developments. From this unfulfilled reformation of the Church, from this being bogged halfway between

Catholicism and the New Testament Church organization, a series of important conclusions can be drawn. The one who alone expends and who stands up before the whole congregation is essentially teacher and administrator of the Sacrament. For only teaching and administration of the Sacrament, not other spiritual functions, give rise to this setting of clergy and laity over against each other. The pastor justifies his sole responsibility for doctrine through his monopoly of theological training, his being set apart with a view to administering the Sacrament by means of his monopoly of canonical ordination. Both move in the direction of an ecclesiastical Objectivism after the Catholic pattern. This Objectivism comes to a clear expression above all in the acceptance of the anti-Donatist propositions in the Augsburg Confession.

On the basis of the Catholic idea of the Church it is logical to explain that the dispensing of salvation is wholly independent from the person of the ecclesiastical giver, the bearer of the office. We are dealing after all with an *opus operatum*, with a magical-hyperphysical event. The canonical Objectivism of the office and the completely impersonal handling of it belongs to the real Objectivism of the Sacrament, to the holy substance of the Host. The Bible knows nothing of this Objectivism. The Word of God in every age is certainly infinitely superior to the man to whom it is entrusted. By way of exception, God can surely even speak His Word through an unbeliever. But the proclamation is certainly always meant and enjoined to be a testimony of faith — 'I believe, therefore I speak' — and a prophetic happening. Not the moral condition of the bearer of the office as such is constitutive for the delivery of the Word, but ' anointing by the Spirit '; to be armed with the Holy Spirit — which no ordination as a canonical act is able to confer — is decisive for the power of the proclamation. Proclamation is an event of a personal character which moves ' out of faith into faith.' Only he can actually speak the Word who has himself been gripped by it and thereby has also been transformed. An unbeliever can lecture on pure doctrine, and lack of belief detracts in no way from the clarity and Biblical correctness of his doctrine. Doctrine is impersonal-objective, is separable from the person; prophetic proclamation of the Word on the contrary is not. Consequently the anti-Donatist formulas of the Augsburg Confession wholly fail to conform with the genuine Reformation concept of the Word of God and proclamation, but rather to the orthodox objectivization of the concepts of Word, faith, and proclamation. This objectivization, as an invincible residue of the Objectivistic interpretation of the Church, from the beginning kept pace with the Reformation interpretation of the Church, and to an increasing degree usurped the latter's place.

The presentation of pure doctrine requires no spiritual qualifications, but certainly theological study. One could very well be a skilled theologian who could make subtle distinctions between the concepts of pure and corrupt doctrine without having real, living faith. For the mediation of pure doctrine, therefore, a bearer of office who believes is not necessary, but only one who is theologically trained. So the strong emphasis shifts from spiritual-personal to impersonal-intellectual, from genuinely churchly to scholastic. The attempt is made to hide this deficiency of churchly qualification by means of canonical qualifications. Correctly to administer the Sacrament neither a particular amount of theological training nor a real ' anointing by the Spirit ' in the sense of personal faith is necessary, but solely the canonical ordination. One must be *rite vocatus,* lawfully called to his vocation.

Being called to an office in the New Testament — be it apostolic, prophetic, diaconate, or episcopate — is always a highly spiritual happening, an event which takes place between God and man through the Holy Spirit, at times with and at times without human mediation. Of a fixed, impersonal-canonical ordering of this relation there is no trace to be found in the New Testament. It is the sign of clerical transformation when canonical qualifications replace spiritual. Where the first question asked concerns the *rite vocatus* no question is raised about spiritual quality, but simply about concurrence with ecclesiastical law. One must not allow himself to be deceived by the liturgical clothing and theological interpretation of the canonical act of ordination: by gradually transforming the spiritual-personal characteristics to those of the canonical order, the nature of the office becomes something quite other than it was in the New Testament.

The Ecclesiastical Office and Contemporary Man. Two characteristic displacements in Protestantism concerning the office — that from the prophetic-personal Word of God to pure doctrine and that from spiritual to canonical qualification for the office — above all else make the ecclesiastical office questionable for contemporary man. Theological education is not able today to establish a unique ecclesiastical position, in a time when Bibles and education are accessible to everyone. The time when only the ' reverend clergyman ' was able to interpret the Bible is past, however much the labor expended in theological schooling for Biblical interpretation. In accordance with the universal priesthood each member of the congregation fundamentally is at least a reader of the Bible. At the time of the Reformers the practical realization of this principle was precluded by the many delimitations to the educated life. Today these hindrances for the most part have fallen away. The monopoly of position of the theologically educated in the congregation is weakened; the office of the Word must be reconstituted to conform with the New Testament meaning. But the office of administrator of the Sacrament has also outgrown its one-sided canonical basis and constituting; we again require of a priest who as representative governs a priestly congregation more than that he be *rite vocatus,* and can no longer reconcile the calling to office with canonical ordination.

To this we must add a second, positive factor. The general intellectual development of man in modern times has led to the situation that if a man becomes a Christian through God's grace, he can no longer understand being a Christian as merely a passive belonging to a congregation, but he must interpret it (at all odds in the New Testament meaning) as responsibility for the congregation. The contemporary Christian intends to share responsibility, intends to give his strength in the service of the Church, and is disillusioned by the Church if it withholds from him this right of service. A

Church that gives him nothing to do cannot satisfy him. The historical development thus leads the Church back to the position which it was starting to give up at the beginning of the second century and to which even the Reformation was unable to lead it back: to the Church which practically as well as fundamentally was the Church of the universal priesthood of all believers, to the overcoming of the false Objectivistic concept of the office, taken over from the Catholic Church. We cannot foresee in what way the renewing of the New Testament actuality of the congregation will accomplish itself in the individual. But it is certain that such renewing will bring with it a basic transformation of the Church and will have far-reaching consequences for its entire upbuilding and activity. The pastor — that is to say, the believing Christian who has the advantage over the others of a thorough theological training — will also have his necessary place in this newly formed Church; but the time of the 'clergyman-church' is definitely past.

The Pastoral Word. The day of the 'clergyman-church' is past for the single reason that it is no longer able to meet the spiritual needs of our time. It is somewhat astonishing in what measure the apostles, who 'turned the world upside down' with their message and whose word in an incomparable way had the character of a public proclamation to the whole world, dedicated themselves to pastoral work with the individual. 'I never stopped,' said Paul in taking leave of the Ephesians, ' to admonish *each one of you with tears day and night.*' The most intense pastoral work directed to the indi-

vidual by the man who proselytized half the world and established countless congregations! The contemporary pastor of
a large city, and sometimes even more the pastor of a small
city or large village, must feel ashamed in the face of the
Pauline injunction, 'Admonishing every one with tears.'
What can pastoral work mean in our congregations of four
and more thousand souls! But the Apostle Paul assures us
throughout all the Epistles that public proclamation without
personal pastoral work is not to be justified. Should this hold
valid less today than in those times — today, with a people
spoiled and conditioned by Individualism and psychology,
who no longer attend public preaching services and are no
longer able to understand the Word to all as the Word to the
individual?

Once again this is an Objectivistic interpretation of the
Word of God which has no understanding of the individual
cure of souls. The presentation of doctrine does not necessarily require personal ministry to the individual. What is
said to all can equally meet the need of the individual because
of its conceptual clarity — logic and grammar are the same for
all persons. Why should one say particularly to the individual what one has already said so plainly on Sunday to all
together? Pastoral work is taken seriously only when one
knows that delivering the Word of God is something other
than presenting pure doctrine, that to the delivering of the
divine Word belongs the will that this Word should take
possession of man, should lead him 'to the obedience of
faith'; hence when concern about the Word is also concern
about its being impressed upon and having it mold the indi-

vidual. Pastoral work is proclamation interpreted in love to the individual. It goes back therefore in a wholly special measure and in a unique way to the proclamation of God's Word which has the quality of a person and the characteristics of an experience, as the Bible time and again shows us. Most of the discourses of Jesus are thus not general proclamation — ' Let whoever will, hear ' — but pastoral conversation. Similarly, the Word of God delivered by the prophet is frequently a message to an individual person. Nathan did not deliver a catechetical sermon to King David. By divine commission he spoke the Word of God to him as a highly personal pastoral word. The fundamental Biblical relation of personal correspondence between the Word of God and the human answer becomes especially apparent in such pastoral care.

Thanks to its Objectivistic tradition, our Church is very poorly endowed for such pastoral care. Quite apart from the fact that the almost exclusively scientific preparation for the ministerial office does not create the most favorable conditions for the pastoral activity, the number of pastors in contrast to the number of those who need the *cura specialis* — and according to Paul everyone needs just that! — is ridiculously small. The Church, if it wishes to discharge its pastoral duties even in a measure, urgently needs lay workers. In pastoral service too the universal priesthood attains its highest realization, for here the individual spiritual experience and personal familiarity with the Bible is of much greater import than scientific-theological studies, while the public interpretation of Scripture in the sermon demands special schooling. But, contrariwise, a sermon which develops out of

lay pastoral work could be called, in a quite different way from
the present day, preaching in the name of the congregation.
A genuine sermon not **only** creates spiritual fellowship but
must grow out of it.

The Objectivized Church. In conclusion, I should like to
link together what we have now come to recognize in three
aspects as false Objectivism in the Church with what was said
earlier about the difference between personal and institutional
Church. Whenever the Church is not understood primarily
as fellowship, but as ' establishment,' as institution, as ' something,' it is objectivized in a false way. This objectivization
occurred on the part of the Reformation Church because in
the proclamation of the Word of God pure doctrine, and in
the Sacrament the factor of administration in perfect form,
was emphasized first and foremost, if not exclusively. This
occurred already in the early days of the Reformation through
Melanchthon's linking the objective characteristics of the
Church, pure doctrine and correct administration of the Sacrament, with the definition of the essence of the Church in
the Augsburg Confession. The question about the characteristics of the true Church is definitely legitimate and necessary;
the New Testament time and again speaks of them. Yet it is
certainly of little value to consider pure doctrine and correct
administration of the Sacrament as such characteristics; but
— one thinks for example of the standards which the Epistles
applied to the congregations — the quality of the daily life
of the members, expressed in numerous ways, must prove
whether God's living Word is present and efficacious in a con-

gregation. But Melanchthon by the marks of a true Church understood something quite different: objective criteria, iron-clad, disposable standards. As such, pure doctrine and correct administration of the Sacrament offer themselves to him. In contrast to the living Word of God, both can be fixed, at least in a measure, once for all, and like a standard meter, a disposable measure, manipulated. From the correct proposition, ' The true Church is and becomes everywhere where the Word of God is livingly present,' the false proposition was formulated: The true Church can be discerned through the existence of right doctrine and the correct administration of the Sacrament. With this *quid pro quo* a second is linked: the concept ' characteristic of the true Church ' is connected by means of a clarifying relative sentence so closely with the concept ' essence of the Church ' that the misunderstanding was almost unavoidable, namely, that pure doctrine and correct administration of the Sacrament *constitute the essential concept of the Church*. In this way the personal concept of the Church — which is the only New Testament one — is obscured by the Objectivist concept of institution; and the revolutionary perception of Luther — that the Church is nothing other than a fellowship of persons, namely, the believers who through their present Lord, their Head, are connected with a body — was again lost. In place of the two-sided concept of the Church, which expresses personal correspondence — the Church is the fellowship of believers which is grounded in God's Word — the one-sided Objectivist concept entered: The Church exists wherever pure doctrine is proclaimed. This proposition, altogether false, one can now trace as the principal proposition throughout the entire doctrine of the post-Reformation Church — as if there were not also a proclamation of God's Word which did not immediately awaken faith and hence did not create a Church. The false, one-sided objective concept of the Church is certainly also to blame for the Church's no longer understanding itself as a missionary Church.

The reduction to two of the criteria for the true Church given us in the New Testament, and indeed to the two which offer themselves most easily to objectivization, namely, pure doctrine and correct administration of the Sacrament, resulted in the period following in a tremendous impoverishment of the Church. The New Testament provided standards for congregations to examine themselves with respect to their being genuine Churches: whether they held fast to the Word, whether they were in obedience, whether their faith was alive, whether they were fruitful in the works of love, steadfast in bearing suffering, zealous in service for the Lord, joined together in true brotherly love and mutual admonition. While this personal correspondence of Word of God and obedience-in-faith is precisely the genuine object of self-testing, everything is now limited to the two objective criteria which characterize the Church as institution but not as fellowship of faith. That the Church turned so much toward doctrine, so little toward discipleship, is a chief reason for its weakness, which is now becoming apparent. A Church that detaches itself from the world only in speaking, even if it were speaking in the purest Biblical doctrine, but not in action and love, becomes unworthy of belief to the world. It deserves such a condemnation as the Bible has already clearly pointed out. One-sided Objectivism, since its beginning the genuine inner danger of the Church, must work particularly destructively in the Church of the Reformation, which grew out of the struggle against this very Objectivism.

We are at the end. It has proved fruitful to us, we hope, to explore the entire range of the Church and its theology with the searchlight of the concepts of Objectivism and Subjectivism and so to test their understanding of Biblical truth. The right to do this we have taken from the Bible itself, in which all truth is understood as the truth of a relationship, namely, the relation of personal correspondence between the Word of God and human obedience-in-faith. With this concept of personal correspondence we did not compass any kind of rational principle, grounded in itself and understood by itself; but we comprehended that which forces itself upon the mind of the observant Bible reader as common denominator of all Biblical proclamation, which is indissolubly linked with the Biblical understanding of God and the Biblical history of revelation. That the Biblical understanding of truth is ' historical ' is an old notion. The meaning of this historicity we have tried to understand anew on the basis of the Bible itself as the truth which is superior to the Object-Subject antithesis and the rational concept of truth determined by it. The truth of which the Bible speaks is always a happening, and indeed the happening of the meeting between God and man, an act of God which must be received by an act of man. The truth acting — this is the characteristic unphilosophical, non-Greek way in which the Bible speaks of truth. In the measure that this understanding of truth again becomes alive in it, the Church will itself be renewed again into the true Church. For this renascence we are hoping.

INDEX

II. Index of Names